Leveled
Text-Dependent
Question
Stems

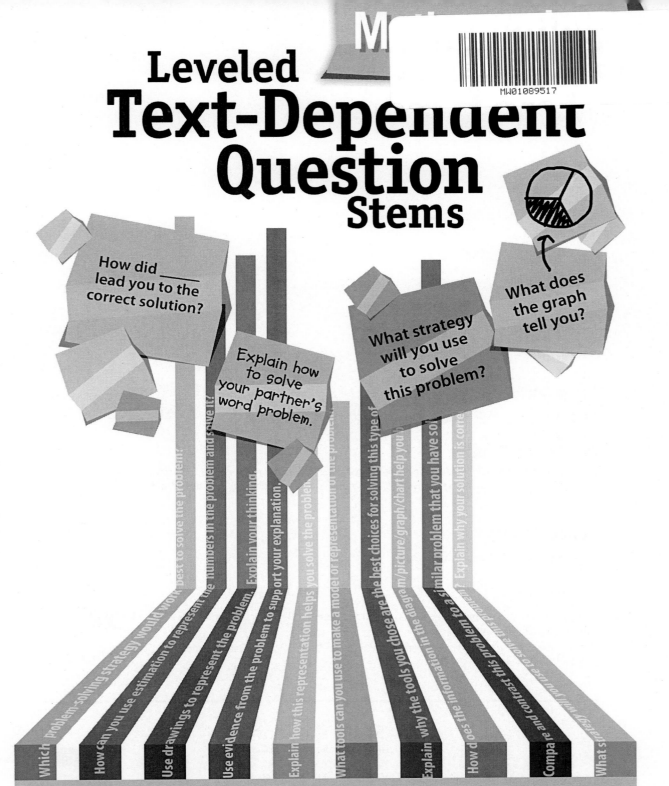

How did ___ lead you to the correct solution?

Explain how to solve your partner's word problem.

What strategy will you use to solve this problem?

What does the graph tell you?

Which problem-solving strategy would work best to solve the problem?

How can you use estimation to represent the numbers in the problem and solve it?

Use drawings to represent the problem.

Use evidence from the problem to support your explanation.

Explain how this representation helps you solve the problem

What tools can you use to make a model or representation of the problem

Explain why the tools you chose are the best choices for solving this type of

How does the information in the diagram/picture/graph/chart help you

Compare and contrast this problem to a similar problem that you have so

What strategy will your solution is corre

Explain why your solution is corre

Authors

Lisa M. Sill, M.A.Ed.

Donna Ventura, M.A.Ed.

SHELL EDUCATION

Contributing Author

Jodene Lynn Smith, M.A.

Publishing Credits

Corinne Burton, M.A.Ed., *President*; Conni Medina, M.A.Ed., *Managing Editor*; Emily R. Smith, M.A.Ed., *Content Director*; Lee Aucoin, *Senior Graphic Designer*; Lynette Ordoñez, *Editor*; Stephanie Bernard, *Assistant Editor*

Image Credits

All images from iStock and Shutterstock.

Standards

© Copyright 2010. National Governors Association Center for Best Practices and Council of Chief State School Officers. All right reserved.

© 2007 Board of Regents of the University of Wisconsin System. World-Class Instructional Design and Assessment (WIDA)

Shell Education

A division of Teacher Created Materials
5301 Oceanus Drive
Huntington Beach, CA 92649-1030
www.tcmpub.com/shell-education

ISBN 978-1-4258-1644-5

© 2017 Shell Educational Publishing, Inc.

Table of Contents

What Are Text-Dependent Questions?

From literary novels and dramas, to textbooks, word problems, newspaper articles, scientific reports, primary sources, and websites, texts vary in content and style. Regardless of the format, students must be able to decode and comprehend the contents of the texts to learn from the material. Text-dependent questions (TDQs) increase students' understanding through in-depth examinations of particular aspects of the texts. They guide students to examine specific portions of the texts and then provide evidence for their answers. Unlike other types of questions, TDQs rely solely on the text so that students may not necessarily need to access significant background knowledge or include outside information.

TDQs facilitate the comprehension of text on a variety of levels. On the most specific level, these questions help students analyze words and sentences within the text to determine the specific meanings and connotations of particular words and phrases. TDQs also enable students to study broader concepts, such as text structure and point of view. They aid students in their study of the individuals, settings, and sequences of events in a text and provide a means for investigating the presence of other types of media within the writing (e.g., drawings, illustrations, graphs, tables). These questions offer an effective tool for helping students analyze the overarching themes, concepts, arguments, and claims presented in texts. TDQs help students build their abilities to compare multiple texts to each other on a variety of topics. Through thoughtful design and sequencing, TDQs can be tailored to meet many specific educational standards and learning objectives while still maintaining a direct connection to the text.

Leveled Text-Dependent Questions

Leveling TDQs helps teachers differentiate content to allow all students access to the concepts being explored. While the TDQ stems are written at a variety of levels, each level remains strong in focusing on the content and vocabulary presented in the texts. Teachers can focus on the same content standard or objective for the whole class, but individual students can access the texts at their independent instructional levels rather than at their frustration levels.

Teachers can also use the TDQs as scaffolds for teaching students. At the beginning of the year, students at the lowest reading levels may need focused teacher guidance as they respond to the questions. As the year progresses, teachers can begin giving students multiple levels of the same questions to aid them in improving their comprehension independently. By scaffolding the content in this way, teachers can support students as they move up through the thinking levels.

What Are Text-Dependent Questions? *(cont.)*

Creating TDQs

This book offers 480 text-dependent question stems that can be used to increase reading comprehension in mathematics problem solving. Each question stem can be slightly altered to ask the type of question you need. However, it may be necessary to create other TDQs to supplement or support the ones supplied in this book.

When considering what type of TDQ to ask, it is important to think about the key ideas in the text or problem and the desired outcomes of the lesson. What should students understand at the end of the lesson? What are the core concepts of the text or problem? Once these main ideas and objectives have been identified, teachers can determine the particular aspects of the text or problem that should be studied for students to reach these goals. Examine key vocabulary words that are related to the underlying core concepts, and develop questions that highlight these connections. Furthermore, identify complex sections of the text or problem that may prove difficult for students, and create questions that allow students to address and master the comprehension challenges presented by the text or problem.

It is also important to consider the sequence of the TDQs presented to students. Generally, the opening questions should be straightforward, giving students the opportunity to become familiar with the text or problem and removing any technical obstacles, such as challenging vocabulary words, which could hinder comprehension. After students gain a basic understanding, introduce more complex questions that strive to illuminate the finer, more intricate concepts. By scaffolding the questions to move from basic, concrete topics to elaborate, implied concepts, you can use TDQs to guide students to a detailed understanding of the complexities of a text or problem.

The key to making sure that questions are dependent on the text is to think about the answer. Can the answer be found in the text, or is an inference created based on facts in the text? If the answer is anchored to the text in some way, it is a strong TDQ!

Setting the Stage for Text and Problem Analysis

When using questioning strategies for analysis, it is vital to establish a safe and collaborative classroom environment. TDQs are designed to stimulate critical-thinking skills and increase reading comprehension in all content areas. It is building these skills, not getting the "right answer," that is the ultimate goal, and students may need to be reminded of this fact. Many TDQs are open ended and don't have single, correct answers. To ensure a collaborative classroom environment, students need to be confident that their answers to questions and their contributions to classroom discussions will be respected by everyone in the room.

TDQs Across the Content Areas

It is usually regarded as the task of the English or language arts teacher to guide students through the effective use of comprehension strategies as they read. Although students read in almost every subject area they study, some teachers may overlook the need to guide students through comprehension tasks with textbooks, word problems, or nonfiction pieces. Comprehension strategies best serve students when they are employed across the curricula and in the context of their actual learning. It is only then that students can independently use the strategies successfully while reading. Students will spend the majority of their adulthoods reading nonfiction expository writing. With this in mind, teachers at all levels must actively pursue ways to enhance their students' abilities to understand reading material. Utilizing TDQs specific to mathematics content is one way to achieve this goal.

TDQs can be used to facilitate the comprehension and understanding of any type of text. These strategies can, and should, be applied to any type of text across disciplines and content areas. For example, mathematics word problems provide excellent opportunities for the use of TDQs in the mathematics classroom. Analyzing mathematical problems and the thinking required to solve these problems offer ample opportunity for in-depth study through TDQs.

Twenty-first Century Literacy Demands

The literacy demands of the twenty-first century are tremendous. Literacy was defined a century ago by one's ability to write his or her own name. In the 1940s, one needed to be able to read at the eighth-grade level to function adequately in the factory setting. To be considered literate today, one needs to be able to read text written at high school levels as a part of workplace and civic duties and leisure activities.

Students and teachers today have entered a new era in education—one that is deeply tied to the technological advances that permeate the modern world. Today, some children can use cell phones to take pictures before they learn to talk. Students in school use the Internet and online libraries to access information from remote locations. Now more than ever, it is the content-area teacher's responsibility to prepare students for the diverse and rigorous reading demands of our technological age. To become effective and efficient readers, students must utilize comprehension strategies automatically and independently. Students need teacher guidance to help them become independent readers and learners so that they not only understand what they read but also question it and explore beyond it.

TDQs Across the Content Areas (cont.)

Integrating Literacy and Mathematics

The goal of literacy in mathematics is to develop students' curiosity about the world around them. Students must observe, ask questions, and then search to find the answers to those questions. Students usually look to their textbooks, often the only books they have for mathematics instruction, to find the answers to their questions. But, this confines them to a realm that is often too abstract to understand. Today's students do not necessarily understand the significant role that mathematics plays in their adult lives, and they rarely see the link between reading and mathematics. By continually applying appropriate reading strategies in mathematics, students are able to bridge the gap between the two constructs and ultimately unite them for a better understanding of both.

Using TDQs within Mathematics

To support learning in mathematics, it is important to provide a variety of texts and word problems on different mathematics topics. Look for mathematics trade books, and provide reading materials for a wide range of reading skills. Some students read at a much lower level than others, so include many picture books in addition to articles from mathematics journals. Students will be better able to incorporate their new learning through independent reading into their existing prior knowledge if the materials are organized in terms of the different mathematics strands.

Well-crafted TDQs can help support rich mathematical tasks. Rich tasks provide a framework for students to explore mathematical problems deeply. They should allow students to approach problems and represent solutions in multiple ways. They should be engaging, real-life situations that require students to make decisions and collaborate. Perhaps most importantly, rich tasks have multiple levels, to both challenge above-level learners, and be accessible for below-level learners.

The focus of the question stems in this book is problem solving. These questions are intended to help teachers work through complex word problems with their students. Rather than handing students questions and expecting them to analyze, reflect, and respond on their own, teachers should use TDQs like those in this book to guide their students. Through guided problem solving, students will learn the steps and processes for effective analysis of mathematics problems.

Note
Throughout this book, the term *text* is used in the leveled text-dependent question stems to refer to informational texts, word problems, graphs, charts, and so on. When presenting the questions to students, teachers should substitute the specific type of text for that word. The examples illustrate how to do this.

Skills and Descriptions

Literacy-Based Skill	Description	Page
Analyzing Meaning and Making a Plan	Students analyze mathematical problems to determine their meanings and create plans to solve them.	10
Understanding Numbers and Relative Units	Students consider the relationships among the numbers and the standard or relative units used in problems.	22
Moving from Concrete to Abstract Thinking	Students move from using concrete representations of numbers and problems to more abstract representations.	34
Identifying and Using Appropriate Tools	Students identify and use appropriate tools to solve mathematical problems.	46
Applying Properties of Operations	Students become familiar with the properties of operations and how they affect various types of mathematical problems.	58
Using Problem-Solving Strategies	Students use a variety of problem-solving strategies to analyze and solve problems.	70
Forming Mathematical Conjectures	Students formulate, discuss, and evaluate mathematical conjectures.	82
Communicating Mathematical Thinking	Students communicate their mathematical thinking visually, orally, and through writing.	94
Considering Ideas of Others	Students carefully consider the ideas of others and apply new ideas and perspectives to their own work.	106
Justifying Strategies, Processes, and Solutions	Students justify and defend why their strategies, processes, and solutions are reasonable and accurate.	118
Creating Word Problems	Students create interesting and challenging word problems to solve and share with others.	130
Discovering Mathematics in the Real World	Students identify mathematical ideas in the real world and explain how mathematical concepts might be used in real-world situations.	142

How to Use This Book

Skill Overview—Each skill is defined on the first page of its section. This explains what the skill is and how to introduce it to students.

Complexity—The text-dependent question stems in this book are differentiated to four complexity levels. The levels roughly correlate to four grade ranges as follows:

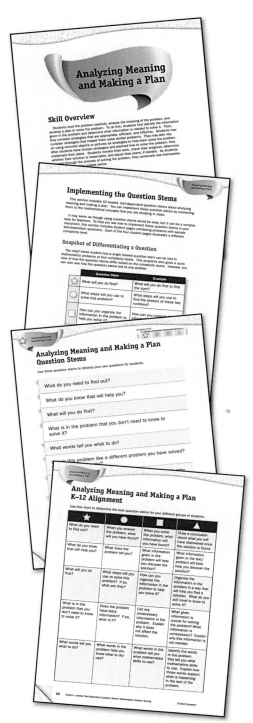

- ☆   grades K–1
- ○   grades 2–4
- ▢   grades 5–8
- △   grades 9–12

Implementing the Question Stems—The second page of each section contains an example question stem differentiated to all four complexity levels. This is a great way for teachers to see a model of how the leveled text-dependent questions can be used with their students.

Question Stems—Each of the 12 sections includes 10 question stems differentiated to four complexity levels for a total of 480 questions in the book. Along with a chart showing the 10 question stems, each complexity level also includes leveled word problems with sample text-dependent questions.

K–12 Alignment—The final two pages in each section include the leveled text-dependent question stems in one chart. This allows teachers to use these two pages to differentiate the text-dependent questions for their students.

Analyzing Meaning and Making a Plan

Skill Overview

Students read problems carefully, analyze their meanings, and develop plans to solve them. To do this, students first identify the information given in problems and determine what information is needed to solve them. Then, they consider strategies that are appropriate, efficient, and effective. Students may consider strategies that helped them solve similar problems. They may also rely on using concrete objects or pictures as strategies to help them solve problems. After students have chosen strategies and created plans, they implement their plans. Students monitor their work, check their progress, determine whether their solutions are reasonable, and adjust their plans, if needed. As students proceed through the process of solving problems, they continually ask themselves whether their solutions make sense.

Implementing the Question Stems

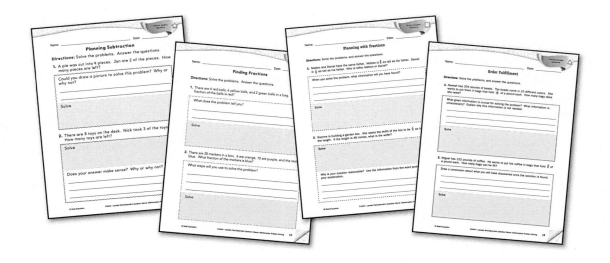

This section includes 10 leveled, text-dependent question stems about analyzing meaning and making a plan. You can implement these question stems by connecting them to the mathematical concepts that you are studying in class.

It may seem as though using question stems would be easy, but it can be a complex task for teachers. To help you see how to implement these question stems in your classroom, this section includes student pages containing problems with sample text-dependent questions. Each of the four student pages illustrates a different complexity level.

Snapshot of Differentiating a Question

The chart below models how a single leveled question stem can be tied to mathematics problems at four complexity levels. This snapshot also gives a quick view of how the question stems differ based on the complexity levels. However, you can also see how the question stems link to one another.

	Question Stem	Example
☆	What will you do first?	What will you do first to find the sum?
○	What steps will you take to solve this problem?	What steps will you take to find the product of these two numbers?
☐	How can you organize the information in the problem to help you solve it?	How can you organize the information in the problem to help you solve for x?
△	Organize the information in the problem in a way that will help you solve it. What do you still need to know to solve it?	Organize the information in the problem in a way that will help you solve it. What do you still need to know to write and solve an equation?

Analyzing Meaning and Making a Plan Question Stems

Use these question stems to develop your own questions for students.

What do you need to find out?

What do you know that will help you?

What will you do first?

What is in the problem that you don't need to know to solve it?

What words tell you what to do?

How is this problem like a different problem you have solved? How can that help you?

Could you use _____ (*strategy*) to solve this problem? Why or why not?

What does the picture/graph/chart tell you?

What do you think the answer will be? Would this answer make sense? Why or why not?

Does your answer make sense? Why or why not?

Name: _____ Date: _____

Planning Subtraction

Directions: Solve the problems. Answer the questions.

1. A pie was cut into 4 pieces. Jan ate 2 of the pieces. How many pieces are left?

> Could you draw a picture to solve this problem? Why or why not?
>
> _____
>
> _____
>
> Solve

2. There are 8 toys on the desk. Nick took 3 of the toys. How many toys are left?

> Solve
>
> Does your answer make sense? Why or why not?
>
> _____
>
> _____
>
> _____

LOW · HIGH

Analyzing Meaning and Making a Plan Question Stems

Use these question stems to develop your own questions for students.

When you answer the problem, what will you have found?

What does the problem tell you?

What steps will you take to solve this problem?

Does the problem have extra information? If so, what is it?

What words in the problem help you know what to do/use?

Is there another problem that you solved that is similar to this one? How can that help you?

Tell why you would not use _____ (*strategy*) to solve this problem. How does knowing this help you?

How does the diagram/picture/graph/chart help you?

Estimate an answer. Does your estimate make sense? Do you need to use a different strategy? Why or why not?

Is your answer reasonable? How do you know?

Name: _____ Date: _____

Finding Fractions

Directions: Solve the problems. Answer the questions.

1. There are 4 red balls, 6 yellow balls, and 2 green balls in a bag. What fraction of the balls is red?

What does the problem tell you?

_____

_____

Solve

2. There are 20 markers in a box. 6 are orange, 10 are purple, and the rest are blue. What fraction of the markers is blue?

What steps will you take to solve this problem?

_____

_____

_____

Solve

Analyzing Meaning and Making a Plan Question Stems

Use these question stems to develop your own questions for students.

When you solve the problem, what information will you have found?

What information given in the problem will help you solve it?

How can you organize the information in the problem to help you solve it?

List any unnecessary information in the problem. Explain why it does not affect the solution.

What words in the problem tell you what mathematics skills to use?

What strategies have you used to solve similar problems? How might they apply to this problem?

Explain why you would not use _____ (*strategy*) to solve this problem. How does thinking about this lead you to a better strategy?

How does the information in the diagram/picture/graph/chart help you better understand the problem?

Estimate a solution using a strategy that you are considering. Explain why you would or would not use this strategy to solve the problem.

Why is your solution reasonable? Use the information from the problem in your explanation.

Name: _____ Date: _____

Planning with Fractions

Directions: Solve the problems, and answer the questions.

1. Matteo and Daniel have the same father. Matteo is $\frac{4}{5}$ as tall as their father. Daniel is $\frac{7}{9}$ as tall as their father. Who is taller, Matteo or Daniel?

> When you solve the problem, what information will you have found?
>
> _____
>
> _____
>
> _____
>
> Solve

2. Gwynne is building a garden box. She wants the width of the box to be $\frac{1}{3}$ as long as the length. If the length is 48 inches, what is the width?

> Solve
>
> Why is your solution reasonable? Use the information from the word problem in your explanation.
>
> _____
>
> _____
>
> _____

Analyzing Meaning and Making a Plan Question Stems

Use these question stems to develop your own questions for students.

Draw a conclusion about what you will have discovered once the solution is found.

What information given in the problem will best help you find the solution?

Organize the information in the problem in a way that will help you solve it. What do you still need to know to solve it?

What given information is crucial for solving the problem? What information is unnecessary? Explain why this information is not needed.

Identify the words in the problem that tell you what mathematics skills to use. Explain how those words support your understanding.

Compare and contrast this problem with a similar problem. Include how the strategies used to solve the other problem might help you solve this one.

Explain why you would not use _____ (*strategy*) to solve this problem. How does considering this lead you to a better strategy?

Evaluate how the information in the diagram/picture/graph/chart helps you better understand the problem.

Estimate a solution using a strategy that you are considering. Evaluate whether or not you should use this strategy to solve the problem.

Demonstrate that your solution makes sense. Use information from the problem in your explanation.

Name: _____ Date: _____

Order Fulfillment

Directions: Solve the problems, and answer the questions.

1. Neveah has 204 pounds of beads. The beads come in 10 different colors. She wants to put them in bags that hold $\frac{1}{12}$ of a pound each. How many bags does she need?

What given information is crucial for solving the problem? What information is unnecessary? Explain why this information is not needed.

_____

_____

_____

Solve

---

2. Miguel has 152 pounds of coffee. He wants to put the coffee in bags that hold $\frac{3}{4}$ of a pound each. How many bags can he fill?

Draw a conclusion about what you will have discovered once the solution is found.

_____

_____

_____

Solve

Analyzing Meaning and Making a Plan
K–12 Alignment

Use this chart to determine the best question stems for your different groups of students.

★	●	■	▲
What do you need to find out?	When you answer the problem, what will you have found?	When you solve the problem, what information will you have found?	Draw a conclusion about what you will have discovered once the solution is found.
What do you know that will help you?	What does the problem tell you?	What information given in the problem will help you solve it?	What information given in the problem will best help you find the solution?
What will you do first?	What steps will you take to solve this problem?	How can you organize the information in the problem to help you solve it?	Organize the information in the problem in a way that will help you solve it. What do you still need to know to solve it?
What is in the problem that you don't need to know to solve it?	Does the problem have extra information? If so, what is it?	List any unnecessary information in the problem. Explain why it does not affect the solution.	What given information is crucial for solving the problem? What information is unnecessary? Explain why this information is not needed.
What words tell you what to do?	What words in the problem help you know what to do/use?	What words in the problem tell you what mathematics skills to use?	Identify the words in the problem that tell you what mathematics skills to use. Explain how those words support your understanding.

Analyzing Meaning and Making a Plan
K–12 Alignment (cont.)

★	●	■	▲
How is this problem like a different problem you have solved? How can that help you?	Is there another problem that you solved that is similar to this one? How can that help you?	What strategies have you used to solve similar problems? How might they apply to this problem?	Compare and contrast this problem with a similar problem. Include how the strategies used to solve the other problem might help you solve this one.
Could you use _____ (strategy) to solve this problem? Why or why not?	Tell why you would not use _____ (strategy) to solve this problem. How does knowing this help you?	Explain why you would not use _____ (strategy) to solve this problem. How does thinking about this lead you to a better strategy?	Explain why you would not use _____ (strategy) to solve this problem. How does considering this lead you to a better strategy?
What does the picture/graph/chart tell you?	How does the diagram/picture/graph/chart help you?	How does the information in the diagram/picture/graph/chart help you better understand the problem?	Evaluate how the information in the diagram/picture/graph/chart helps you better understand the problem.
What do you think the answer will be? Would this answer make sense? Why or why not?	Estimate an answer. Does your estimate make sense? Do you need to use a different strategy? Why or why not?	Estimate a solution using a strategy that you are considering. Explain why you would or would not use this strategy to solve the problem.	Estimate a solution using a strategy that you are considering. Evaluate whether or not you should use this strategy to solve the problem.
Does your answer make sense? Why or why not?	Is your answer reasonable? How do you know?	Why is your solution reasonable? Use the information from the problem in your explanation.	Demonstrate that your solution makes sense. Use information from the problem in your explanation.

Understanding Numbers and Relative Units

Skill Overview

Before solving problems, students take ample time to understand the numbers and the relative units. They consider the relationships these numbers and units have to their solutions. Students ask themselves whether the numbers in the solutions should be greater than, equal to, or less than the numbers given in the problems. As students solve problems, they consider the numbers and the units involved in each step. Students should be sure that their strategies, computations, and answers reflect the meanings of the problems. By ensuring that the relative units and numbers are correct, students demonstrate that they understand the meanings behind the problems and what the problems are asking.

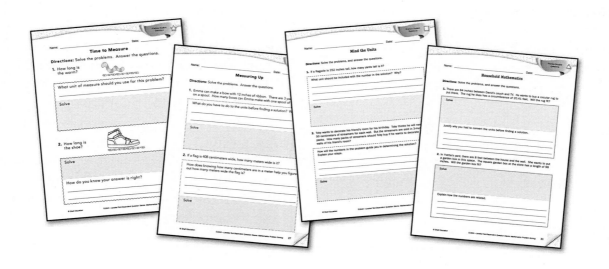

Implementing the Question Stems

This section includes 10 leveled, text-dependent question stems about numbers and relative units. You can implement these question stems by connecting them to the mathematical concepts that you are studying in class.

It may seem as though using question stems would be easy, but it can be a complex task for teachers. To help you see how to implement these question stems in your classroom, this section includes student pages containing problems with sample text-dependent questions. Each of the four student pages illustrates a different complexity level.

Snapshot of Differentiating a Question

The chart below models how a single leveled question stem can be tied to mathematics problems at four complexity levels. This snapshot also gives a quick view of how the question stems differ based on the complexity levels. However, you can also see how the question stems link to one another.

	Question Stem	Example
☆	What number tells you how many _____ (unit) there are?	What number tells you how many blocks there are?
○	What number represents how many _____ (unit) there are?	What number represents how many centimeters there are?
☐	What does each number in the problem represent?	What does each number in the equation represent?
△	Explain what each number in the problem represents.	Explain what each number in the equation represents.

COMPLEXITY

LOW ☆ ● ■ ▲ HIGH

Understanding Numbers and Relative Units Question Stems

Use these question stems to develop your own questions for students.

What is the unit? How do you know?

What do you know that can help you?

What number tells you how many _____ (*unit*) there are?

What do you know about the units?

Are there things in the problem that can be changed? If so, what are they?

Make an estimate. Why do you think this is a good estimate?

Think about the numbers in the problem. What will you do first?

How do you know your answer is right?

What is the same about _____ (*number*) and _____ (*number*)?

What unit of measure should you use for this problem?

Name: _____   Date: _____

Time to Measure

Directions: Solve the problems. Answer the questions.

1. How long is the worm?

What unit of measure should you use for this problem?

_____

Solve

2. How long is the shoe?

Solve

How do you know your answer is right?

_____

_____

Understanding Numbers and Relative Units Question Stems

Use these question stems to develop your own questions for students.

What unit(s) are you working with? Why?

How does knowing _____ (*unit/concept*), help you figure out _____ (*unit/concept*)?

What number represents how many _____ (*unit*) there are?

What do you have to do to the units before finding a solution? Why?

What in the problem can be changed? What cannot be changed?

Make an estimate. Explain why your estimate is reasonable.

Think about the numbers in the problem and how you will use them. List the steps you will take.

How do you know that you have solved the problem correctly?

What is the same about _____ (*number*) and _____ (*number*)? What is different?

What would the correct unit of measure be for this problem? Explain your thinking.

Name: _____ Date: _____

Measuring Up

Directions: Solve the problems. Answer the questions.

1. Emma can make a bow with 12 inches of ribbon. There are 3 yards of ribbon
   on a spool. How many bows can Emma make with one spool of ribbon?

   What do you have to do to the units before finding a solution? Why?

   _____

   _____

   Solve

2. If a flag is 408 centimeters wide, how many meters wide is it?

   How does knowing how many centimeters are in a meter help you figure
   out how many meters wide the flag is?

   _____

   _____

   _____

   Solve

Understanding Numbers and Relative Units Question Stems

Use these question stems to develop your own questions for students.

What unit(s) should be included with the number(s) in the solution? Why?

How does knowing _____ (*unit/concept*) help you determine _____ (*unit/concept*)?

What does each number in the problem represent?

Why do you have to convert the units in the problem?

What is the constant in the problem, and what is the variable?

Estimate a solution. Defend why your estimate is reasonable.

How will the numbers in the problem guide you in determining the solution? Explain your steps.

Explain why your solution is correct. Use evidence from the problem to support your explanation.

How are the numbers in the problem related?

Explain how you know the correct unit of measure for this problem.

Name: _____ Date: _____

Mind the Units

Directions: Solve the problems, and answer the questions.

1. If a flagpole is 252 inches tall, how many yards tall is it?

> What unit should be included with the number in the solution? Why?
>
> _____
>
> _____
>
> _____
>
> Solve

2. Toby wants to decorate his friend's room for his birthday. Toby thinks he will need 50 centimeters of streamers for each wall. But the streamers are sold in 3-meter packs. How many packs of streamers should Toby buy if he wants to decorate all four walls of his friend's room?

> How will the numbers in the problem guide you in determining the solution? Explain your steps.
>
> _____
>
> _____
>
> _____
>
> Solve

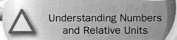

Understanding Numbers and Relative Units Question Stems

Use these question stems to develop your own questions for students.

Justify what unit(s) should be included with the number(s) in the solution. Explain how you came to that conclusion.

Explain how knowing _____ (*unit/concept*) can help you determine _____ (*unit/concept*).

Explain what each number in the problem represents.

Justify why you have to convert the units before finding a solution.

Determine the constant and the variable in the problem.

Estimate a solution. How does it compare to the numbers given? Defend why your estimate is reasonable.

Describe the steps you will take and how the numbers in the problem will guide you in determining the solution.

Use evidence from the problem to justify why your solution is correct.

Explain how the numbers in the problem and the solution are related.

Use evidence from the problem to explain how you know the appropriate unit of measure.

Name: _____ Date: _____

Household Mathematics

Directions: Solve the problems, and answer the questions.

1. There are 84 inches between David's couch and TV. He wants to buy a circular rug to put there. The rug he likes has a circumference of 20.41 feet. Will the rug fit?

> Solve
>
>
>
>
>
> Justify why you had to convert the units before finding a solution.
>
> _____
>
> _____
>
> _____

2. In Yvette's yard, there are 8 feet between the house and the wall. She wants to put a garden box in this space. The square garden box at the store has a length of 98 inches. Will the garden box fit?

> Solve
>
>
>
>
>
> Explain how the numbers are related.
>
> _____
>
> _____
>
> _____

Understanding Numbers and Relative Units K–12 Alignment

Use this chart to determine the best question stems for your different groups of students.

★	●	■	▲
What is the unit? How do you know?	What unit(s) are you working with? Why?	What unit(s) should be included with the number(s) in the solution? Why?	Justify what unit(s) should be included with the number(s) in the solution. Explain how you came to that conclusion.
What do you know that can help you?	How does knowing _____ (*unit/concept*) help you figure out _____ (*unit/concept*)?	How does knowing _____ (*unit/concept*) help you determine _____ (*unit/concept*)?	Explain how knowing _____ (*unit/concept*) can help you determine _____ (*unit/concept*).
What number tells you how many _____ (*unit*) there are?	What number represents how many _____ (*unit*) there are?	What does each number in the problem represent?	Explain what each number in the problem represents.
What do you know about the units?	What do you have to do to the units before finding a solution? Why?	Why do you have to convert the units in the problem?	Justify why you have to convert the units before finding a solution.
Are there things in the problem that can be changed? If so, what are they?	What in the problem can be changed? What cannot be changed?	What is the constant in the problem, and what is the variable?	Determine the constant and the variable in the problem.

Understanding Numbers and Relative Units
K–12 Alignment *(cont.)*

⭐	⚫	⬛	🔺
Make an estimate. Why do you think this is a good estimate?	Make an estimate. Explain why your estimate is reasonable.	Estimate a solution. Defend why your estimate is reasonable.	Estimate a solution. How does it compare to the numbers given? Defend why your estimate is reasonable.
Think about the numbers in the problem. What will you do first?	Think about the numbers in the problem and how you will use them. List the steps you will take.	How will the numbers in the problem guide you in determining the solution? Explain your steps.	Describe the steps you will take and how the numbers in the problem will guide you in determining the solution.
How do you know your answer is right?	How do you know that you have solved the problem correctly?	Explain why your solution is correct. Use evidence from the problem to support your explanation.	Use evidence from the problem to justify why your solution is correct.
What is the same about _____ (number) and _____ (number)?	What is the same about _____ (number) and _____ (number)? What is different?	How are the numbers in the problem related?	Explain how the numbers in the problem and the solution are related.
What unit of measure should you use for this problem?	What would the correct unit of measure be for this problem? Explain your thinking.	Explain how you know the correct unit of measure for this problem.	Use evidence from the problem to explain how you know the appropriate unit of measure.

Moving from Concrete to Abstract Thinking

Skill Overview

Students progress from using various types of concrete models to increasingly abstract models to represent and solve problems. Initially, students use concrete models such as blocks, counters, objects, or tiles. Then, as they gain understanding, they represent problems through figures, drawings, diagrams, tables, or graphs. Finally, students develop and use abstract thinking and reasoning. They represent problems symbolically through numeric or algebraic expressions and equations. Types of abstract models range from addition, subtraction, multiplication, or division number sentences, to algebraic expressions and equations, proportional relationships, and mathematical functions. Throughout the process, students monitor their work to ensure their models are appropriate for the problems and their solutions are reasonable. Students may modify or adjust their strategies and models as needed.

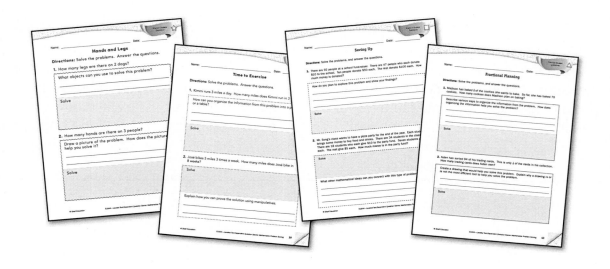

Implementing the Question Stems

This section includes 10 leveled, text-dependent question stems about moving to more abstract thinking. You can implement these question stems by connecting them to the mathematical concepts that you are studying in class.

It may seem as though using question stems would be easy, but it can be a complex task for teachers. To help you see how to implement these question stems in your classroom, this section includes student pages containing problems with sample text-dependent questions. Each of the four student pages illustrates a different complexity level.

Snapshot of Differentiating a Question

The chart below models how a single leveled question stem can be tied to mathematics problems at four complexity levels. This snapshot also gives a quick view of how the question stems differ based on the complexity levels. However, you can also see how the question stems link to one another.

	Question Stem	Example
☆	How does your model/ picture/table show the numbers in the problem?	How does your picture show the numbers in the problem?
○	How does your model/ picture/table represent the numbers in the problem?	How does your model represent the numbers in the problem?
▢	Explain how your model/ picture/table represents the numbers in the problem.	Explain how your table represents the numbers in the problem.
△	Defend how your model/ picture/table accurately represents the numbers in the problem.	Defend how your model accurately represents the numbers in the problem.

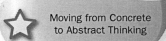

Moving from Concrete to Abstract Thinking Question Stems

Use these question stems to develop your own questions for students.

What objects can you use to solve this problem?

How do the _____ (*manipulative*) show the answer?

How does your model/picture/table show the numbers in the problem?

What kind of drawing would help you solve this problem?

Draw a picture of the problem. How does the picture help you solve it?

What is your plan for this problem? How can you show your answer?

What other mathematics topics does this make you think of?

Do the number sentence and the model match? How?

Can you put what you know in a picture or a table? How?

Use the picture/table to write a number sentence.

Name: _____   Date: _____

Hands and Legs

Directions: Solve the problems. Answer the questions.

1. How many legs are there on 2 dogs?

> What objects can you use to solve this problem?
>
> _____
>
> _____
>
> Solve

2. How many hands are there on 3 people?

> Draw a picture of the problem. How does the picture help you solve it?
>
> _____
>
> _____
>
> Solve

Moving from Concrete to Abstract Thinking Question Stems

Use these question stems to develop your own questions for students.

What manipulatives could you use to model this problem? Why would that be a good choice for the problem?

Explain how you can prove the answer using manipulatives.

How does your model/picture/table represent the numbers in the problem?

Draw a picture that would help you solve this problem.

Draw a model of the problem. How does the model help you solve it?

What is your plan for solving this problem? How can you show your findings?

Can you connect this problem with any other mathematical ideas? How?

How do the number sentence and the model match?

How can you organize the information from this problem into a picture or a table?

What number sentence can be written from this picture/table? Explain how the number sentence represents the picture/table.

Name: _____ Date: _____

Time to Exercise

Directions: Solve the problems. Answer the questions.

1. Kimmi runs 3 miles a day. How many miles does Kimmi run in 3 weeks?

> How can you organize the information from this problem into a picture or a table?
>
> _____
>
> _____
>
> Solve

2. José bikes 5 miles 3 times a week. How many miles does José bike in 8 weeks?

> Solve
>
> Explain how you can prove the answer using manipulatives.
>
> _____
>
> _____

© Shell Education   51644—Leveled Text-Dependent Question Stems: Mathematics Problem Solving   **39**

Moving from Concrete to Abstract Thinking Question Stems

Use these question stems to develop your own questions for students.

How could you use manipulatives to represent this problem? Explain why you used the manipulative you chose.

How can you justify your solution using manipulatives?

Explain how your model/picture/table represents the numbers in the problem.

Draw examples of pictures that would help you solve this problem.

Use drawings to represent the problem. Explain how this representation helps you solve the problem.

How do you plan to explore this problem and show your findings?

What other mathematical ideas can you connect with this type of problem?

Describe how the number sentence is related to the model.

Describe how you can organize the information from the problem.

What number sentence can be written from this picture/table? Explain how your number sentence accurately represents the picture/table.

Name: _____ Date: _____

Saving Up

Directions: Solve the problems, and answer the questions.

1. There are 92 people at a school fund-raiser. There are 47 people who each donate $10 to the school. Ten people donate $50 each. The rest donate $100 each. How much money is donated?

How do you plan to explore this problem and show your findings?

_____

_____

_____

Solve

2. Mr. Song's class wants to have a pizza party for the end of the year. Each student brings some money to buy food and drinks. There are 34 students in the class. There are 18 students who each give $10 to the party fund. Seven students give $6 each. The rest give $5 each. How much money is in the party fund?

Solve

What other mathematical ideas can you connect with this type of problem?

_____

_____

_____

Moving from Concrete to Abstract Thinking Question Stems

Use these question stems to develop your own questions for students.

How could you represent this problem using manipulatives? Explain why the manipulative you chose is the best tool to model this problem.

Use manipulatives to justify your solution. Explain how the manipulatives you chose are effective tools for modeling the problem.

Defend how your model/picture/table accurately represents the numbers in the problem.

Create a drawing that would help you solve this problem. Explain why a drawing is or is not the most efficient tool to help you solve the problem.

Draw a representation of the problem. Explain how this accurately represents the problem and how it can help you solve it.

Develop a plan for how you will explore this problem and show your findings.

Describe any other mathematical ideas you can connect with this problem.

Explain the relationship between the number sentence and the model.

Describe various ways to organize the information from the problem. How does organizing the information help you solve it?

How can you create a number sentence from this picture/table? Justify how your number sentence is an accurate representation of the picture/table.

Name: _____ Date: _____

Fractional Planning

Directions: Solve the problems, and answer the questions.

1. Madison has baked $\frac{2}{3}$ of the cookies she wants to bake. So far, she has baked 70 cookies. How many cookies does Madison plan on baking?

> Describe various ways to organize the information from the problem. How does organizing the information help you solve it?
>
> _____
>
> _____
>
> _____
>
> Solve

2. Aiden has sorted 94 of his trading cards. This is only $\frac{1}{5}$ of the cards in his collection. How many trading cards does Aiden own?

> Create a drawing that would help you solve this problem. Explain why a drawing is or is not the most efficient tool to help you solve the problem.
>
> _____
>
> _____
>
> _____
>
> Solve

Moving from Concrete to Abstract Thinking K–12 Alignment

Use this chart to determine the best question stems for your different groups of students.

★	●	■	▲
What objects can you use to solve this problem?	What manipulatives could you use to model this problem? Why would that be a good choice for the problem?	How could you use manipulatives to represent this problem? Explain why you used the manipulative you chose.	How could you represent this problem using manipulatives? Explain why the manipulative you chose is the best tool to model this problem.
How do the _____ (*manipulative*) show the answer?	Explain how you can prove the answer using manipulatives.	How can you justify your solution using manipulatives?	Use manipulatives to justify your solution. Explain how the manipulatives you chose are effective tools for modeling the problem.
How does your model/picture/table show the numbers in the problem?	How does your model/picture/table represent the numbers in the problem?	Explain how your model/picture/table represents the numbers in the problem.	Defend how your model/picture/table accurately represents the numbers in the problem.
What kind of drawing would help you solve this problem?	Draw a picture that would help you solve this problem.	Draw examples of pictures that would help you solve this problem.	Create a drawing that would help you solve this problem. Explain why a drawing is or is not the most efficient tool to help you solve the problem.
Draw a picture of the problem. How does the picture help you solve it?	Draw a model of the problem. How does the model help you solve it?	Use drawings to represent the problem. Explain how this representation helps you solve the problem.	Draw a representation of the problem. Explain how this accurately represents the problem and how it can help you solve it.

Moving from Concrete to Abstract Thinking
K–12 Alignment *(cont.)*

★	●	■	▲
What is your plan for this problem? How can you show your answer?	What is your plan for solving this problem? How can you show your findings?	How do you plan to explore this problem and show your findings?	Develop a plan for how you will explore this problem and show your findings.
What other mathematics topics does this make you think of?	Can you connect this problem with any other mathematical ideas? How?	What other mathematical ideas can you connect with this type of problem?	Describe any other mathematical ideas you can connect with this problem.
Do the number sentence and the model match? How?	How do the number sentence and the model match?	Describe how the number sentence is related to the model.	Explain the relationship between the number sentence and the model.
Can you put what you know in a picture or a table? How?	How can you organize the information from this problem into a picture or a table?	Describe how you can organize the information from the problem.	Describe various ways to organize the information from the problem. How does organizing the information help you solve it?
Use the picture/table to write a number sentence.	What number sentence can be written from this picture/table? Explain how the number sentence represents the picture/table.	What number sentence can be written from this picture/table? Explain how your number sentence accurately represents the picture/table.	How can you create a number sentence from this picture/table? Justify how your number sentence is an accurate representation of the picture/table.

Identifying and Using Appropriate Tools

Skill Overview

Students identify and use grade-appropriate tools to help them find reasonable solutions. Students use manipulatives, such as counters, coins, and base-ten blocks, to make problems more concrete. They use tools, such as calculators, standard and non-standard measurement tools, straight edges, protractors, and compasses. They may use tally marks, spinners, number cubes, and other tools for statistical problems. Students use computer software and various programs to visualize the results of different assumptions, examine and compare the results, and arrive at reasonable conclusions. Students should also use approximations and estimations to find and verify solutions. Students will become more confident, efficient, and skilled as they continue to explore problems in which they need to use tools, estimations, and approximations.

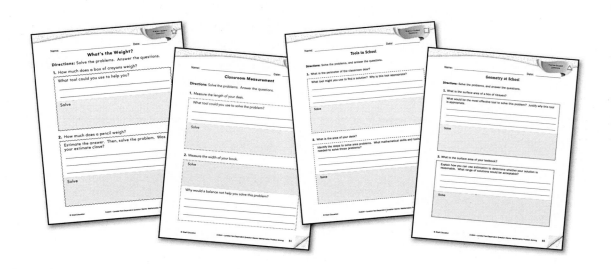

Implementing the Question Stems

This section includes 10 leveled, text-dependent question stems about identifying and using appropriate tools. You can implement these question stems by connecting them to the mathematical concepts that you are studying in class.

It may seem as though using question stems would be easy, but it can be a complex task for teachers. To help you see how to implement these question stems in your classroom, this section includes student pages containing problems with sample text-dependent questions. Each of the four student pages illustrates a different complexity level.

Snapshot of Differentiating a Question

The chart below models how a single leveled question stem can be tied to mathematics problems at four complexity levels. This snapshot also gives a quick view of how the question stems differ based on the complexity levels. However, you can also see how the question stems link to one another.

	Question Stem	Example
☆	How would _____ (tool) help you?	How would counters help you?
◯	How can you use _____ (tool) to solve the problem?	How can you use base-ten blocks to solve the problem?
▢	Explain how _____ (tool) can help you solve the problem. Why is this the right tool to use?	Explain how a spreadsheet program can help you solve the problem. Why is this the right tool to use?
△	Explain why _____ (tool) is the appropriate tool to solve this problem, and describe how it will help you solve it.	Explain why a graphing calculator is the appropriate tool to solve this problem, and describe how it will help you solve it.

Identifying and Using Appropriate Tools Question Stems

Use these question stems to develop your own questions for students.

How would _____ (*tool*) help you?

Estimate the answer. Then, solve the problem. Was your estimate close?

How can you use _____ (*tool*) to show your answer?

What tool could you use to help you?

What tool would you use to measure this?

Would _____ (*tool*) be a good tool to solve this problem? Why or why not?

What do you have to do to solve this problem? What tools do you need?

Can you estimate to tell whether your answer is right? How?

What tools can you use to show the problem?

What objects can you use to help solve the problem?

Name: _____ Date: _____

What's the Weight?

Directions: Solve the problems. Answer the questions.

1. How much does a box of crayons weigh?

What tool could you use to help you?

_____

_____

Solve

2. How much does a pencil weigh?

Estimate the answer. Then, solve the problem. Was your estimate close?

_____

_____

_____

Solve

LOW   HIGH

Identifying and Using Appropriate Tools Question Stems

Use these question stems to develop your own questions for students.

How can you use _____ (*tool*) to solve the problem?

Estimate a solution. How does this help you solve the problem?

How can you use _____ (*tool*) to prove your answer is correct?

What tool could you use to solve the problem?

What tool would you use to measure this? Why?

Why would _____ (*tool*) not help you solve this problem?

List the steps to solve _____ (*type of problem*) problems. What tools are needed to solve them?

How can you use estimation to tell whether your answer is reasonable?

What tools can you use to make a model of the problem?

What manipulatives could help you solve the problem?

Name: _____ Date: _____

Classroom Measurement

Directions: Solve the problems. Answer the questions.

1. Measure the length of your desk.

What tool could you use to solve the problem?

_____

_____

Solve

2. Measure the width of your book.

Solve

Why would a balance not help you solve this problem?

_____

_____

_____

Identifying and Using Appropriate Tools Question Stems

Use these question stems to develop your own questions for students.

Explain how _____ (*tool*) can help you solve the problem. Why is this the right tool to use?

How can you use estimation to represent the numbers in the problem and solve it?

How can you use _____ (*tool*) to verify that your solution is correct?

What tool might you use to find a solution? Why is this tool appropriate?

Explain what tool you would use to measure this. Why is this the best measurement tool for the problem?

Explain why _____ (*tool*) would not be a helpful tool to solve this problem.

Identify the steps to solve _____ (*type of problem*) problems. What mathematical skills and tools are needed to solve them?

How can you use estimation to determine whether your solution is reasonable?

What tools can you use to make a model of the problem? Explain why these tools are the best choices for solving this problem.

Explain what manipulative would help you solve the problem and why it is the best choice for this problem.

Name: _____ Date: _____

Tools in School

Directions: Solve the problems, and answer the questions.

1. What is the perimeter of the classroom door?

What tool might you use to find a solution? Why is this tool appropriate?

_____

_____

_____

Solve

2. What is the area of your desk?

Identify the steps to solve area problems. What mathematical skills and tools are
needed to solve them?

_____

_____

_____

Solve

Identifying and Using Appropriate Tools Question Stems

Use these question stems to develop your own questions for students.

Explain why _____ (*tool*) is the appropriate tool to solve this problem, and describe how it will help you solve it.

How can you use estimation to test your strategy before you solve it? Explain why this step is beneficial.

Explain how can you use _____ (*tool*) to verify that your solution is correct and reasonable.

What would be the most effective tool to solve this problem? Justify why this tool is appropriate.

Describe various tools you could use to measure this. Explain which would be the best measurement tool for the problem and why.

Explain why _____ (*tool*) would not be a helpful tool to solve this problem. Identify a tool that would be more helpful and explain why.

Identify the steps to solve _____ (*type of problem*) problems. List the mathematical skills and tools that are needed in order to solve them.

Explain how you can use estimation to determine whether your solution is reasonable. What range of solutions would be acceptable?

What tools can you use to make a model of the problem? Justify why the tools you selected are appropriate for this type of problem.

Explain what manipulative would best help you solve the problem. Justify why it is the most appropriate choice.

Name: _____ Date: _____

Geometry at School

Directions: Solve the problems, and answer the questions.

1. What is the surface area of a box of tissues?

> What would be the most effective tool to solve this problem? Justify why this tool
> is appropriate.
>
> _____
>
> _____
>
> _____
>
> Solve

2. What is the surface area of your textbook?

> Explain how you can use estimation to determine whether your solution is
> reasonable. What range of solutions would be acceptable?
>
> _____
>
> _____
>
> _____
>
> Solve

Identifying and Using Appropriate Tools
K–12 Alignment

Use this chart to determine the best question stems for your different groups of students.

★	●	■	▲
How would _____ (tool) help you?	How can you use _____ (tool) to solve the problem?	Explain how _____ (tool) can help you solve the problem. Why is this the right tool to use?	Explain why _____ (tool) is the appropriate tool to solve this problem, and describe how it will help you solve it.
Estimate the answer. Then, solve the problem. Was your estimate close?	Estimate a solution. How does this help you solve the problem?	How can you use estimation to represent the numbers in the problem and solve it?	How can you use estimation to test your strategy before you solve it? Explain why this step is beneficial.
How can you use _____ (tool) to show your answer?	How can you use _____ (tool) to prove your answer is correct?	How can you use _____ (tool) to verify that your solution is correct?	Explain how can you use _____ (tool) to verify that your solution is correct and reasonable.
What tool could you use to help you?	What tool could you use to solve the problem?	What tool might you use to find a solution? Why is this tool appropriate?	What would be the most effective tool to solve this problem? Justify why this tool is appropriate.
What tool would you use to measure this?	What tool would you use to measure this? Why?	Explain what tool you would use to measure this. Why is this the best measurement tool for the problem?	Describe various tools you could use to measure this. Explain which would be the best measurement tool for the problem and why.

Identifying and Using Appropriate Tools
K–12 Alignment *(cont.)*

⭐	⚫	◻	🔺
Would _____ (*tool*) be a good tool to solve this problem? Why or why not?	Why would _____ (*tool*) not help you solve this problem?	Explain why _____ (*tool*) would not be a helpful tool to solve this problem.	Explain why _____ (*tool*) would not be a helpful tool to solve this problem. Identify a tool that would be more helpful and explain why.
What do you have to do to solve this problem? What tools do you need?	List the steps to solve _____ (*type of problem*) problems. What tools are needed to solve them?	Identify the steps to solve _____ (*type of problem*) problems. What mathematical skills and tools are needed to solve them?	Identify the steps to solve _____ (*type of problem*) problems. List the mathematical skills and tools that are needed in order to solve them.
Can you estimate to tell whether your answer is right? How?	How can you use estimation to tell whether your answer is reasonable?	How can you use estimation to determine whether your solution is reasonable?	Explain how you can use estimation to determine whether your solution is reasonable. What range of solutions would be acceptable?
What tools can you use to show the problem?	What tools can you use to make a model of the problem?	What tools can you use to make a model of the problem? Explain why these tools are the best choices for solving this problem.	What tools can you use to make a model of the problem? Justify why the tools you selected are appropriate for this type of problem.
What objects can you use to help solve the problem?	What manipulatives could help you solve the problem?	Explain what manipulative would help you solve the problem and why it is the best choice for this problem.	Explain what manipulative would best help you solve the problem. Justify why it is the most appropriate choice.

Applying Properties of Operations

Skill Overview

The properties of operations for both addition and multiplication are the commutative property, the associative property, the distributive property, and the identity property. By applying these properties, students will understand a logical and consistent approach to solving problems. As students become familiar with each property of operation, they describe the property and provide examples of problems that require its application. Students explain the solutions to problems through the use of the properties of operations. They also understand why these properties cannot be used in other operations, such as subtraction and division. This understanding helps students apply higher-order thinking skills to various types of mathematical problems. It also ensures that students truly understand how different operations affect numbers and equations.

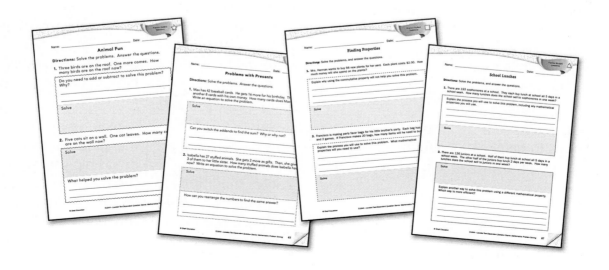

Implementing the Question Stems

This section includes 10 leveled, text-dependent question stems about applying the properties of operations. You can implement these question stems by connecting them to the mathematical concepts that you are studying in class.

It may seem as though using question stems would be easy, but it can be a complex task for teachers. To help you see how to implement these question stems in your classroom, this section includes student pages containing problems with sample text-dependent questions. Each of the four student pages illustrates a different complexity level.

Snapshot of Differentiating a Question

The chart below models how a single leveled question stem can be tied to mathematics problems at four complexity levels. This snapshot also gives a quick view of how the question stems differ based on the complexity levels. However, you can also see how the question stems link to one another.

	Question Stem	Example
☆	Do you need to add, subtract, multiply, or divide to solve this problem? Why?	Do you need to add, subtract, multiply, or divide to solve this problem? Why?
○	Why is it important to know _____ (*operation*) to solve this problem?	Why is it important to know subtraction to solve this problem?
☐	How does understanding the _____ (*mathematical property*) help you solve this problem?	How does understanding the commutative property help you solve this problem?
△	Provide specific examples of how understanding the _____ (*mathematical property*) helps you solve this problem.	Provide specific examples of how understanding the distributive property helps you solve this problem.

Applying Properties of Operations Question Stems

Use these question stems to develop your own questions for students.

How did you know to _____ (*operation*)?

What steps will you take to solve the problem?

Do you need to add, subtract, multiply, or divide to solve this problem? Why?

What can you learn about _____ (*operation*) from this problem?

Why can't you use _____ (*operation*) to solve this problem?

What helped you solve the problem?

How can you switch the numbers to find the sum?

How can you switch the numbers to make a 10?

What other numbers would have the same sum/product?

Is there a different way to solve this problem?

Name: _____ Date: _____

Animal Fun

Directions: Solve the problems. Answer the questions.

1. Three birds are on the roof. One more comes. How many birds are on the roof now?

> Do you need to add or subtract to solve this problem? Why?
>
> _____
>
> _____
>
> Solve

2. Five cats sit on a wall. One cat leaves. How many cats are on the wall now?

> Solve
>
> What helped you solve the problem?
>
> _____
>
> _____

Applying Properties of Operations Question Stems

Use these question stems to develop your own questions for students.

How did you know to use _____ (*operation*) to solve the problem?

What steps will you take to solve the problem? What operations will you need to use?

Why is it important to know _____ (*operation*) to solve this problem?

How does this problem help you better understand _____ (*operation*)?

Why can't _____ (*operation*) be used to solve this problem?

What mathematical ideas helped you solve this problem?

Can you switch the addends to find the sum? Why or why not?

How can you rearrange the numbers to find the same answer?

How can you change the numbers and still get the same product?

Describe another way you could solve this problem.

Name: _____ Date: _____

Problems with Presents

Directions: Solve the problems. Answer the questions.

1. Max has 42 baseball cards. He gets 16 more for his birthday. Then, he buys another 8 cards with his own money. How many cards does Max have now? Write an equation to solve the problem.

> Solve
>
>
> Can you switch the addends to find the sum? Why or why not?
>
> _____
>
> _____

2. Isabella has 27 stuffed animals. She gets 2 more as gifts. Then, she gives 3 of them to her little sister. How many stuffed animals does Isabella have now? Write an equation to solve the problem.

> Solve
>
>
> How can you rearrange the numbers to find the same answer?
>
> _____
>
> _____

Applying Properties of Operations Question Stems

Use these question stems to develop your own questions for students.

How did you know to use the _____ (*mathematical property*) when solving this problem?

Explain the process you will use to solve this problem. What mathematical properties will you need to use?

How does understanding the _____ (*mathematical property*) help you solve this problem?

What mathematical property do you understand better after solving this problem? Why?

Explain why using the _____ (*mathematical property*) will not help you solve this problem.

Explain how the _____ (*mathematical property*) helped you solve this problem.

Can you switch the addends and get the same sum? Can you do this with other operations? Explain your thinking.

Is it possible to rearrange the numbers to find the sum more easily? Why or why not?

How can you break apart the numbers to find the product?

Is there another mathematical property you could use to solve this problem? Why or why not?

Name: _____ Date: _____

Finding Properties

Directions: Solve the problems, and answer the questions.

1. Mrs. Herman wants to buy 56 new plants for her yard. Each plant costs $2.00. How much money will she spend on the plants?

> Explain why using the distributive property will not help you solve this problem.
>
> _____
>
> _____
>
> _____
>
> Solve

2. Francisco is making party favor bags for his little brother's party. Each bag has 5 toys and 2 games. If Francisco makes 20 bags, how many total items will he need to buy?

> Explain the process you will use to solve this problem. What mathematical properties will you need to use?
>
> _____
>
> _____
>
> _____
>
> Solve

Applying Properties of Operations Question Stems

Use these question stems to develop your own questions for students.

What evidence in the problem helped you decide to use the _____ (*mathematical property*) to solve this problem?

Explain the process you will use to solve this problem, including any mathematical properties you will use.

Provide specific examples of how understanding the _____ (*mathematical property*) helps you solve this problem.

Explain how solving this problem helps you better understand a mathematical property. Use the problem to explain how.

Use examples to justify why using the _____ (*mathematical property*) will not help you solve this problem.

Justify your use of the _____ (*mathematical property*) in solving this problem.

Explain how the commutative property does/does not apply to this problem and why.

Explain how the associative property does/does not apply to this problem and why.

Use the distributive property to explain how these numbers can be broken apart to find the same product. How does that help you solve the problem?

Explain another way to solve this problem using a different mathematical property. Which way is more efficient?

Name: _____ Date: _____

School Lunches

Directions: Solve the problems, and answer the questions.

1. There are 193 sophomores at a school. They each buy lunch at school all 5 days in a school week. How many lunches does the school sell to sophomores in one week?

Explain the process you will use to solve this problem, including any mathematical properties you will use.

_____

_____

_____

Solve

2. There are 136 juniors at a school. Half of them buy lunch at school all 5 days in a school week. The other half of the juniors buy lunch 2 days per week. How many lunches does the school sell to juniors in one week?

Solve

Explain another way to solve this problem using a different mathematical property. Which way is more efficient?

_____

_____

_____

_____

Applying Properties of Operations
K–12 Alignment

Use this chart to determine the best question stems for your different groups of students.

★	●	■	▲
How did you know to _____ (operation)?	How did you know to use _____ (operation) to solve the problem?	How did you know to use the _____ (mathematical property) when solving this problem?	What evidence in the problem helped you decide to use the _____ (mathematical property) to solve this problem?
What steps will you take to solve the problem?	What steps will you take to solve the problem? What operations will you need to use?	Explain the process you will use to solve this problem. What mathematical properties will you need to use?	Explain the process you will use to solve this problem, including any mathematical properties you will use.
Do you need to add, subtract, multiply, or divide to solve this problem? Why?	Why is it important to know _____ (operation) to solve this problem?	How does understanding the _____ (mathematical property) help you solve this problem?	Provide specific examples of how understanding the _____ (mathematical property) helps you solve this problem.
What can you learn about _____ (operation) from this problem?	How does this problem help you better understand _____ (operation)?	What mathematical property do you understand better after solving this problem? Why?	Explain how solving this problem helps you better understand a mathematical property. Use the problem to explain how.
Why can't you use _____ (operation) to solve this problem?	Why can't _____ (operation) be used to solve this problem?	Explain why using the _____ (mathematical property) will not help you solve this problem.	Use examples to justify why using the _____ (mathematical property) will not help you solve this problem.

Applying Properties of Operations
K–12 Alignment (cont.)

★	●	■	▲
What helped you solve the problem?	What mathematical ideas helped you solve this problem?	Explain how the _____ (*mathematical property*) helped you solve this problem.	Justify your use of the _____ (*mathematical property*) in solving this problem.
How can you switch the numbers to find the sum?	Can you switch the addends to find the sum? Why or why not?	Can you switch the addends and get the same sum? Can you do this with other operations? Explain your thinking.	Explain how the commutative property does/does not apply to this problem and why.
How can you switch the numbers to make a 10?	How can you rearrange the numbers to find the same answer?	Is it possible to rearrange the numbers to find the sum more easily? Why or why not?	Explain how the associative property does/does not apply to this problem and why.
What other numbers would have the same sum/product?	How can you change the numbers and still get the same product?	How can you break apart the numbers to find the product?	Use the distributive property to explain how these numbers can be broken apart to find the same product. How does that help you solve the problem?
Is there a different way to solve this problem?	Describe another way you could solve this problem.	Is there another mathematical property you could use to solve this problem? Why or why not?	Explain another way to solve this problem using a different mathematical property. Which way is more efficient?

Using Problem-Solving Strategies

Skill Overview

Students should be given ample opportunities to solve interesting and challenging problems. These problems require thought beyond the use of mathematical algorithms. These types of problems require students to consider their background knowledge and use problem-solving strategies to unlock new knowledge. Examples of strategies include guess and check, using manipulatives, making graphs, drawing the problem, identifying patterns, and working backwards. Page 159 lists additional problem-solving strategies with visuals. This may be used to teach students strategies or serve as a visual reminder of strategies they could try.

Students should work independently or collaborate in groups to solve problems. Students should have opportunities to find solutions multiple times, using a different strategy each time. They will recognize that not all strategies are appropriate to use to solve every problem. Students may feel more comfortable and confident with certain strategies over others.

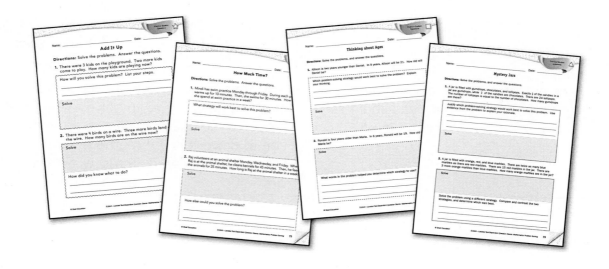

Implementing the Question Stems

This section includes 10 leveled, text-dependent question stems about problem-solving strategies. You can implement these question stems by connecting them to the mathematical concepts that you are studying in class.

It may seem as though using question stems would be easy, but it can be a complex task for teachers. To help you see how to implement these question stems in your classroom, this section includes student pages containing problems with sample text-dependent questions. Each of the four student pages illustrates a different complexity level.

Snapshot of Differentiating a Question

The chart below models how a single leveled question stem can be tied to mathematics problems at four complexity levels. This snapshot also gives a quick view of how the question stems differ based on the complexity levels. However, you can also see how the question stems link to one another.

	Question Stem	Example
☆	How did you know to use _____ (strategy)?	How did you know to use counters?
○	What about the problem convinced you to try _____ (strategy)?	What about the problem convinced you to try drawing the problem?
□	Explain how you decided to use _____ (strategy) to solve this problem.	Explain how you decided to use a chart to solve this problem.
△	Provide evidence from the problem to support your rationale for using _____ (strategy) to solve it.	Provide evidence from the problem to support your rationale for working backwards to solve it.

Using Problem-Solving Strategies Question Stems

Use these question stems to develop your own questions for students.

How could you solve this problem?

How will you solve this problem? List your steps.

Why didn't you _____ (*strategy*) to solve this problem?

Make a plan to solve the problem. How will you solve it?

How did you know to use _____ (*strategy*)?

How else could you solve the problem?

How did you know what to do?

Does _____ (*strategy*) always work for this kind of problem?

How did you solve the problem? When might you use the same steps?

Tell about a different problem that helped you know how to solve this one.

Name: _____ Date: _____

Add It Up

Directions: Solve the problems. Answer the questions.

1. There were 3 kids on the playground. Two more kids come to play. How many kids are playing now?

How will you solve this problem? List your steps.

_____

_____

Solve

2. There were 4 birds on a wire. Three more birds land on the wire. How many birds are on the wire now?

Solve

How did you know what to do?

_____

_____

COMPLEXITY

Using Problem-Solving Strategies Question Stems

Use these question stems to develop your own questions for students.

What strategies could you use to solve this problem?

What strategy will work best to solve this problem?

How did you know not to _____ (*strategy*) to solve the problem?

Make a plan to solve this problem. What strategy will you use?

What about the problem convinced you to try _____ (*strategy*)?

Solve the problem a different way.

What words helped you decide how to solve this problem?

Will _____ (*strategy*) always work in this type of problem? Why or why not?

How did you solve the problem? When else might you use the same strategy?

What did you already know about this type of problem that led you to solve it using this strategy?

Name: _____ Date: _____

How Much Time?

Directions: Solve the problems. Answer the questions.

1. Mindi has swim practice Monday through Friday. During each practice, she warms up for 10 minutes. Then, she swims for 30 minutes. How long does she spend at swim practice in a week?

What strategy will work best to solve this problem?

_____

_____

Solve

2. Raj volunteers at an animal shelter Monday, Wednesday, and Friday. When Raj is at the animal shelter, he cleans kennels for 45 minutes. Then, he feeds the animals for 25 minutes. How long is Raj at the animal shelter in a week?

Solve

Solve the problem a different way.

_____

_____

COMPLEXITY

Using Problem-Solving Strategies Question Stems

Use these question stems to develop your own questions for students.

What are the various problem-solving strategies you could use to solve this problem?

Which problem-solving strategy would work best to solve the problem? Explain your thinking.

Why is _____ (*strategy*) not an effective way to solve this problem?

Create a plan to solve the problem. Explain what strategy you will use and why.

Explain how you decided to use _____ (*strategy*) to solve this problem.

Describe another way to solve this problem. Which strategy is better? Why?

What words in the problem helped you determine which strategy to use?

Will _____ (*strategy*) always work for solving problems similar to this one? Explain why or why not.

Describe how you solved the problem. When else might this be an effective strategy?

Explain how your prior knowledge about this type of problem led you to solve it using this strategy.

Name: _____ Date: _____

Thinking about Ages

Directions: Solve the problems, and answer the questions.

1. Allison is two years younger than Daniel. In 9 years, Allison will be 21. How old will Daniel be?

> Which problem-solving strategy would work best to solve the problem? Explain your thinking.
>
> _____
>
> _____
>
> _____
>
> Solve

2. Ronald is four years older than Maria. In 6 years, Ronald will be 19. How old will Maria be?

> Solve
>
> What words in the problem helped you determine which strategy to use?
>
> _____
>
> _____
>
> _____

Using Problem-Solving Strategies Question Stems

Use these question stems to develop your own questions for students.

Describe the various problem-solving strategies you could use to solve this problem. List the pros and cons of each.

Justify which problem-solving strategy would work best to solve this problem. Use evidence from the problem to explain your rationale.

Explain why _____ (*strategy*) is not an effective problem-solving strategy in this instance.

Create a plan to solve the problem. Explain what strategy you will use and why it is a good choice for this type of problem.

Provide evidence from the problem to support your rationale for using _____ (*strategy*) to solve it.

Solve the problem using a different strategy. Compare and contrast the two strategies, and determine which is best.

What language or details in the problem helped you determine which strategy to use?

Will _____ (*strategy*) always work for solving problems similar to this one? Use details from the problem to explain why or why not.

Explain the strategy you used to solve the problem. When else might this be an effective strategy?

Describe your prior knowledge about this type of problem or a similar one that led you to solve it using this strategy.

Name: _____ Date: _____

Mystery Jars

Directions: Solve the problems, and answer the questions.

1. A jar is filled with gumdrops, chocolates, and lollipops. Exactly $\frac{1}{2}$ of the candies in the jar are gumdrops, while $\frac{1}{4}$ of the candies are chocolates. There are 24 lollipops. How many gumdrops are there?

Justify which problem-solving strategy would work best to solve this problem. Use evidence from the problem to explain your rationale.

_____

_____

_____

Solve

2. A jar is filled with orange, red, and blue marbles. There are twice as many blue marbles as there are red marbles. There are 15 red marbles in the jar. There are 3 more orange marbles than blue marbles. How many orange marbles are in the jar?

Solve

Solve the problem using a different strategy. Compare and contrast the two strategies, and determine which is best.

_____

_____

_____

Using Problem-Solving Strategies
K–12 Alignment

Use this chart to determine the best question stems for your different groups of students.

★	●	■	▲
How could you solve this problem?	What strategies could you use to solve this problem?	What are the various problem-solving strategies you could use to solve this problem?	Describe the various problem-solving strategies you could use to solve this problem. List the pros and cons of each.
How will you solve this problem? List your steps.	What strategy will work best to solve this problem?	Which problem-solving strategy would work best to solve the problem? Explain your thinking.	Justify which problem-solving strategy would work best to solve this problem. Use evidence from the problem to explain your rationale.
Why didn't you _____ (strategy) to solve this problem?	How did you know not to _____ (strategy) to solve the problem?	Why is _____ (strategy) not an effective way to solve this problem?	Explain why _____ (strategy) is not an effective problem-solving strategy in this instance.
Make a plan to solve the problem. How will you solve it?	Make a plan to solve this problem. What strategy will you use?	Create a plan to solve the problem. Explain what strategy you will use and why.	Create a plan to solve the problem. Explain what strategy you will use and why it is a good choice for this type of problem.
How did you know to use _____ (strategy)?	What about the problem convinced you to try _____ (strategy)?	Explain how you decided to use _____ (strategy) to solve this problem.	Provide evidence from the problem to support your rationale for using _____ (strategy) to solve it.

Using Problem-Solving Strategies
K–12 Alignment *(cont.)*

★	●	■	▲
How else could you solve the problem?	Solve the problem a different way.	Describe another way to solve this problem. Which strategy is better? Why?	Solve the problem using a different strategy. Compare and contrast the two strategies, and determine which is best.
How did you know what to do?	What words helped you decide how to solve this problem?	What words in the problem helped you determine which strategy to use?	What language or details in the problem helped you determine which strategy to use?
Does _____ (strategy) always work for this kind of problem?	Will _____ (strategy) always work in this type of problem? Why or why not?	Will _____ (strategy) always work for solving problems similar to this one? Explain why or why not.	Will _____ (strategy) always work for solving problems similar to this one? Use details from the problem to explain why or why not.
How did you solve the problem? When might you use the same steps?	How did you solve the problem? When else might you use the same strategy?	Describe how you solved the problem. When else might this be an effective strategy?	Explain the strategy you used to solve the problem. When else might this be an effective strategy?
Tell about a different problem that helped you know how to solve this one.	What did you already know about this type of problem that led you to solve it using this strategy?	Explain how your prior knowledge about this type of problem led you to solve it using this strategy.	Describe your prior knowledge about this type of problem or a similar one that led you to solve it using this strategy.

Forming Mathematical Conjectures

Skill Overview

Through careful thought, students formulate mathematical conjectures, ideas, and opinions about complex and real-life problems. Students express their mathematical conjectures in concise, logical, and systematic ways orally or through writing. To explain their conjectures, students use models, relate them to previous learning, or use counterexamples. Students identify flaws and errors in their conjectures, revise them, and communicate their new ideas. Students listen to or read the conjectures of others and decide whether they are reasonable and appropriate. Students ask pertinent questions to clarify the thoughts of others, identify flaws and errors, and help others improve their conjectures. This allows students to identify misconceptions and errors in their own thinking, revise their conjectures, and clearly formulate and communicate their final points of view.

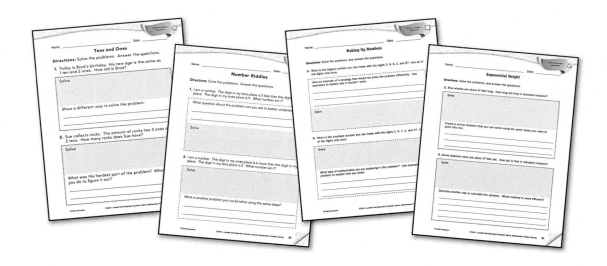

Implementing the Question Stems

This section includes 10 leveled, text-dependent question stems about forming mathematical conjectures. You can implement these question stems by connecting them to the mathematical concepts that you are studying in class.

It may seem as though using question stems would be easy, but it can be a complex task for teachers. To help you see how to implement these question stems in your classroom, this section includes student pages containing problems with sample text-dependent questions. Each of the four student pages illustrates a different complexity level.

Snapshot of Differentiating a Question

The chart below models how a single leveled question stem can be tied to mathematics problems at four complexity levels. This snapshot also gives a quick view of how the question stems differ based on the complexity levels. However, you can also see how the question stems link to one another.

	Question Stem	Example
☆	How did _____ (*strategy/step*) help you?	How did counting the pictures help you?
◯	How did _____ (*strategy/step*) lead you to the correct solution?	How did adding the first two numbers lead you to the correct solution?
▢	Explain how _____ (*strategy/step*) led you to the correct solution.	Explain how dividing by 4 last led you to the correct solution.
△	Evaluate how _____ (*strategy/step*) did or did not lead you to the correct solution.	Evaluate how creating a graph did or did not lead you to the correct solution.

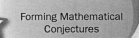

Forming Mathematical Conjectures Question Stems

Use these question stems to develop your own questions for students.

How do you know this is _____ (*type of mathematics*)?

Will your partner's plan work? Why or why not?

What is a question you can ask about the problem?

How did _____ (*strategy/step*) help you?

Show a different way to solve the problem.

What would not be a good way to solve this problem? Why?

How did your model help you solve the problem?

What did your partner say that helped you?

What was the hardest part of the problem? What did you do to figure it out?

Can you follow the same steps/strategy in a different problem? What would that problem look like?

Name: _____ Date: _____

Tens and Ones

Directions: Solve the problems. Answer the questions.

1. Today is Brad's birthday. His new age is the same as 1 ten and 2 ones. How old is Brad?

Solve

Show a different way to solve the problem.

_____

_____

2. Sue collects rocks. The amount of rocks has 3 ones and 2 tens. How many rocks does Sue have?

Solve

What was the hardest part of the problem? What did you do to figure it out?

_____

_____

Forming Mathematical Conjectures Question Stems

Use these question stems to develop your own questions for students.

What type of mathematics are you exploring in this problem? How do you know?

Will your partner's strategy solve the problem? How do you know?

What question about the problem can you ask to better understand it?

How did _____ (*strategy/step*) lead you to the correct solution?

What else could you have done to solve the problem?

What strategy would not solve this problem well? Why?

What did you learn by using a model, and how did it help you solve the problem?

What did your partner say that helped you better understand the problem?

What was the most challenging part of the problem? How did you figure it out?

What is another problem you could solve using the same steps/strategy?

Name: _____ Date: _____

Number Riddles

Directions: Solve the problems. Answer the questions.

1. I am a number. The digit in my tens place is 5 less than the digit in my ones place. The digit in my ones place is 9. What number am I?

What question about the problem can you ask to better understand it?

_____

_____

Solve

2. I am a number. The digit in my ones place is 6 more than the digit in my tens place. The digit in my tens place is 2. What number am I?

Solve

What is another problem you could solve using the same steps?

_____

_____

Forming Mathematical Conjectures Question Stems

Use these question stems to develop your own questions for students.

What type of mathematics are you exploring in this problem? Use examples from the problem to explain how you know.

Will your partner's strategy solve the problem correctly? Explain your thinking.

What questions can you ask to better understand the problem or the mathematical concept?

Explain how _____ (*strategy/step*) led you to the correct solution.

How else might you have calculated the solution?

Give an example of a strategy that would not solve the problem effectively. Use examples to explain why it wouldn't work.

Explain what you learned by using a model to represent and solve the problem. How effective was it?

What kind of feedback did you get from your partner? How did his/her feedback help you better understand the problem?

Explain the most challenging part of the problem and what you did to solve it.

What other types of problems could you solve using these steps/strategies?

Name: _____   Date: _____

Making Up Numbers

Directions: Solve the problems, and answer the questions.

1. What is the largest number you can make with the digits 3, 6, 9, 2, and 8? Use all of the digits only once.

> Give an example of a strategy that would not solve the problem effectively. Use examples to explain why it wouldn't work.
>
> _____
>
> _____
>
> _____
>
> Solve

2. What is the smallest number you can make with the digits 2, 9, 7, 1, and 4? Use all of the digits only once.

> Solve
>
> What type of mathematics are you exploring in this problem? Use examples from the problem to explain how you know.
>
> _____
>
> _____
>
> _____

Forming Mathematical Conjectures Question Stems

Use these question stems to develop your own questions for students.

Describe the type of mathematics you are investigating in this problem. Use specific examples from the problem to explain how you know.

Use examples to prove that your partner's strategy will or will not solve the problem correctly.

What questions can you ask to better understand the problem and further investigate the mathematical concept?

Evaluate how _____ (*strategy/step*) did or did not lead you to the correct solution.

Describe another way to calculate the solution. Which method is more efficient?

Describe a strategy that would not effectively solve this problem. Use specific examples to explain why this strategy would be ineffective.

Explain how using a model to represent and solve the problem affected your understanding of it. How effective was your model?

Evaluate the feedback you received from your partner. How did his/her feedback help you better understand the problem?

Use examples to describe the most challenging part of the problem and how you solved it.

Create a similar problem that you can solve using the same steps/strategies you used to solve this one.

Name: _____   Date: _____

Exponential Height

Directions: Solve the problems, and answer the questions.

1. Blue whales are about 9^2 feet long. How long are they in standard notation?

> Solve
>
>
>
>
>
> Create a similar problem that you can solve using the same steps you used to solve this one.
>
> _____
>
> _____
>
> _____

2. Some redwood trees are about 3^5 feet tall. How tall is that in standard notation?

> Solve
>
>
>
>
>
> Describe another way to calculate the solution. Which method is more efficient?
>
> _____
>
> _____
>
> _____
>
> _____

Forming Mathematical Conjectures K–12 Alignment

Use this chart to determine the best question stems for your different groups of students.

★	●	■	▲
How do you know this is _____ (type of mathematics)?	What type of mathematics are you exploring in this problem? How do you know?	What type of mathematics are you exploring in this problem? Use examples from the problem to explain how you know.	Describe the type of mathematics you are investigating in this problem. Use specific examples from the problem to explain how you know.
Will your partner's plan work? Why or Why not?	Will your partner's strategy solve the problem? How do you know?	Will your partner's strategy solve the problem correctly? Explain your thinking.	Use examples to prove that your partner's strategy will or will not solve the problem correctly.
What is a question you can ask about the problem?	What question about the problem can you ask to better understand it?	What questions can you ask to better understand the problem or the mathematical concept?	What questions can you ask to better understand the problem and further investigate the mathematical concept?
How did _____ (strategy/step) help you?	How did _____ (strategy/step) lead you to the correct solution?	Explain how _____ (strategy/step) led you to the correct solution.	Evaluate how _____ (strategy/step) did or did not lead you to the correct solution.
Show a different way to solve the problem.	What else could you have done to solve the problem?	How else might you have calculated the solution?	Describe another way to calculate the solution. Which method is more efficient?

Forming Mathematical Conjectures
K–12 Alignment *(cont.)*

★	●	■	▲
What would not be a good way to solve this problem? Why?	What strategy would not solve this problem well? Why?	Give an example of a strategy that would not solve the problem effectively. Use examples to explain why it wouldn't work.	Describe a strategy that would not effectively solve this problem. Use specific examples to explain why this strategy would be ineffective.
How did your model help you solve the problem?	What did you learn by using a model, and how did it help you solve the problem?	Explain what you learned by using a model to represent and solve the problem. How effective was it?	Explain how using a model to represent and solve the problem affected your understanding of it. How effective was your model?
What did your partner say that helped you?	What did your partner say that helped you better understand the problem?	What kind of feedback did you get from your partner? How did his/her feedback help you better understand the problem?	Evaluate the feedback you received from your partner. How did his/her feedback help you better understand the problem?
What was the hardest part of the problem? What did you do to figure it out?	What was the most challenging part of the problem? How did you figure it out?	Explain the most challenging part of the problem and what you did to solve it.	Use examples to describe the most challenging part of the problem and how you solved it.
Can you follow the same steps/strategy in a different problem? What would that problem look like?	What is another problem you could solve using the same steps/strategy?	What other types of problems could you solve using these steps/strategies?	Create a similar problem that you can solve using the same steps/strategies you used to solve this one.

Communicating Mathematical Thinking

Skill Overview

In addition to using various strategies to calculate and solve a variety of problems, students must also learn how to communicate their understandings to others. Students communicate their mathematical thinking to precisely explain their ideas, describe their strategies, and justify their answers. Students share their ideas in clear, concise, and convincing manners visually, orally, or in writing. Their communication reflects the use of grade-appropriate mathematical vocabulary, language, and sentence structure.

Through this communication, students gain a better understanding of the meanings behind various mathematical ideas and have a greater likelihood of retaining these ideas. They develop a mathematical language to describe their strategies and processes, to present their solutions, and to explain and justify their answers.

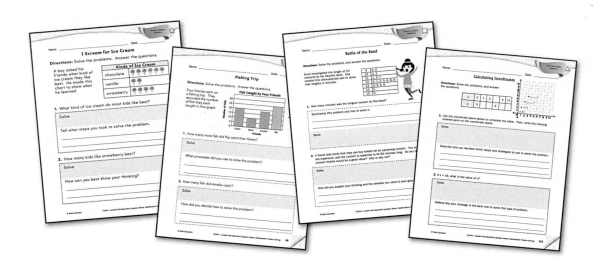

Implementing the Question Stems

This section includes 10 leveled, text-dependent question stems about communicating mathematical thinking. You can implement these question stems by connecting them to the mathematical concepts that you are studying in class.

It may seem as though using question stems would be easy, but it can be a complex task for teachers. To help you see how to implement these question stems in your classroom, this section includes student pages containing problems with sample text-dependent questions. Each of the four student pages illustrates a different complexity level.

Snapshot of Differentiating a Question

The chart below models how a single leveled question stem can be tied to mathematics problems at four complexity levels. This snapshot also gives a quick view of how the question stems differ based on the complexity levels. However, you can also see how the question stems link to one another.

	Question Stem	Example
☆	How can you best show your thinking?	How can you best show your thinking about the number of cars?
○	Why is a table/graph/picture the best way to show your mathematical thinking?	Why is a picture the best way to show your mathematical thinking about subtracting fractions?
☐	Explain why a table/graph/picture is the best way to show your mathematical thinking.	Explain why a table is the best way to show your mathematical thinking about the data.
△	Use examples from the problem to justify why a table/graph/picture is the best way to show your mathematical thinking.	Use examples from the problem to justify why a graph is the best way to show your mathematical thinking about the parabola.

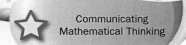

Communicating Mathematical Thinking Question Stems

Use these question stems to develop your own questions for students.

Tell what steps you took to solve the problem.

Was the way you solved the problem the best way? Why?

Tell a partner how to solve the problem.

Draw a picture to show your thinking.

How can you best show your thinking?

What words do you need to know to solve this problem?

How did you tell about your thinking to your group?

Did any of your steps confuse your group?

Why did you solve the problem this way?

If someone else were to solve this problem, what would you tell him or her?

Name: _____ Date: _____

I Scream for Ice Cream

Directions: Solve the problems. Answer the questions.

A boy asked his friends what kind of ice cream they like best. He made this chart to show what he learned.

Kinds of Ice Cream	
chocolate	🍦🍦🍦🍦🍦🍦
vanilla	🍦🍦
strawberry	🍦🍦🍦🍦

1. What kind of ice cream do most kids like best?

Solve
Tell what steps you took to solve the problem.
_____
_____

2. How many kids like strawberry best?

Solve
How can you best show your thinking?
_____
_____

Communicating Mathematical Thinking Question Stems

Use these question stems to develop your own questions for students.

What process did you use to solve the problem?

Why was your strategy the best one to use?

Explain how to solve this problem to another student.

Create a visual to show your thinking.

Why is a table/graph/picture the best way to show your mathematical thinking?

What mathematical terms do you need to know to understand this problem?

How did you explain your thinking to your group?

Did any of your steps confuse your group? How did you explain your steps more clearly to help them understand?

How did you decide how to solve this problem?

If someone else were going to solve this problem, what should he or she look out for?

Name: _____ Date: _____

Fishing Trip

Directions: Solve the problems. Answer the questions.

Four friends went on a fishing trip. They recorded the number of fish they each caught in this graph.

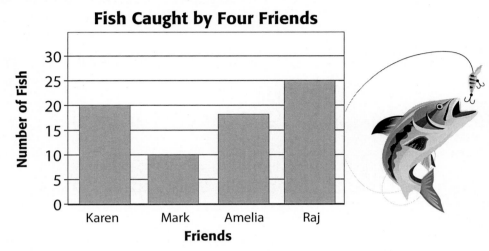

Fish Caught by Four Friends

1. How many more fish did Raj catch than Karen?

Solve

What process did you use to solve the problem?

_____

_____

2. How many fish did Amelia catch?

Solve

How did you decide how to solve this problem?

_____

_____

Communicating Mathematical Thinking Question Stems

Use these question stems to develop your own questions for students.

Describe the process you used to solve the problem.

Explain why the strategy you used is the best strategy.

Summarize this problem and how to solve it.

Create a visual to show your thinking. How does it help explain the problem?

Explain why a table/graph/picture is the best way to show your mathematical thinking.

What mathematical vocabulary do you need to know to understand this problem? Why are those words important?

How did you explain your thinking and the process you used to your group?

What part of your process confused your group? How did you explain it to them so they would understand your thinking?

What did you learn from the problem that helped you decide how to solve it?

If someone else were to solve this problem, what tips would you give him or her?

Name: _____ Date: _____

Battle of the Band

Directions: Solve the problems, and answer the questions.

Emily investigated the length of 20 concerts by her favorite band. She created this stem-and-leaf plot to show their lengths in minutes.

9	0, 6
10	2, 3
11	1, 3, 7
12	0, 1, 2, 5, 6, 8, 8
13	0, 5, 5, 8
14	5
15	0

1. How many minutes was the longest concert by this band?

Summarize this problem and how to solve it.

_____

_____

Solve

2. A friend tells Emily that they can buy tickets for an upcoming concert. The tickets are expensive, and the concert is expected to be 85 minutes long. Do you think the concert tickets would be a good value? Why or why not?

Solve

How did you explain your thinking and the process you used to your group?

_____

_____

LOW · · · · HIGH

Communicating Mathematical Thinking Question Stems

Use these question stems to develop your own questions for students.

Use evidence from the problem to justify the process you used to solve it.

Defend why your strategy is the best one to solve this type of problem.

Summarize this problem and the most effective way to solve it.

Create a visual that effectively shows your understanding of the problem. How does it help explain the problem?

Use examples from the problem to justify why a table/graph/ picture is the best way to show your mathematical thinking.

Explain the mathematical concepts and vocabulary you need to know to understand this problem. Why are those ideas and terms important?

How did you explain your thinking and the process you used to your group? How did you support their understanding of your process?

What part of your process or strategy confused your group? How did you clarify your process so they would understand your thinking?

Describe how you decided which steps and strategies to use to solve the problem.

If someone else were attempting to solve this problem, what advice or tips would you give this person?

Name: _____   Date: _____

Calculating Coordinates

Directions: Solve the problems, and answer
the questions.

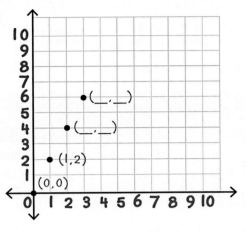

x	0	1	2		4	11
y	0			6		

1. Use the coordinate plane above to complete the table. Then, write the missing
ordered pairs on the coordinate plane.

> Solve
>
>
> Describe how you decided which steps and strategies to use to solve the problem.
>
> _____
>
> _____
>
> _____

2. If $x = 18$, what is the value of y?

> Solve
>
>
> Defend why your strategy is the best one to solve this type of problem.
>
> _____
>
> _____
>
> _____

Communicating Mathematical Thinking K–12 Alignment

Use this chart to determine the best question stems for your different groups of students.

★	●	■	▲
Tell what steps you took to solve the problem.	What process did you use to solve the problem?	Describe the process you used to solve the problem.	Use evidence from the problem to justify the process you used to solve it.
Was the way you solved the problem the best way? Why?	Why was your strategy the best one to use?	Explain why the strategy you used is the best strategy.	Defend why your strategy is the best one to solve this type of problem.
Tell a partner how to solve the problem.	Explain how to solve this problem to another student.	Summarize this problem and how to solve it.	Summarize this problem and the most effective way to solve it.
Draw a picture to show your thinking.	Create a visual to show your thinking.	Create a visual to show your thinking. How does it help explain the problem?	Create a visual that effectively shows your understanding of the problem. How does it help explain the problem?
How can you best show your thinking?	Why is a table/graph/picture the best way to show your mathematical thinking?	Explain why a table/graph/picture is the best way to show your mathematical thinking.	Use examples from the problem to justify why a table/graph/picture is the best way to show your mathematical thinking.

Communicating Mathematical Thinking
K–12 Alignment (cont.)

★	●	■	▲
What words do you need to know to solve this problem?	What mathematical terms do you need to know to understand this problem?	What mathematical vocabulary do you need to know to understand this problem? Why are those words important?	Explain the mathematical concepts and vocabulary you need to know to understand this problem. Why are those ideas and terms important?
How did you tell about your thinking to your group?	How did you explain your thinking to your group?	How did you explain your thinking and the process you used to your group?	How did you explain your thinking and the process you used to your group? How did you support their understanding of your process?
Did any of your steps confuse your group?	Did any of your steps confuse your group? How did you explain your steps more clearly to help them understand?	What part of your process confused your group? How did you explain it to them so they would understand your thinking?	What part of your process or strategy confused your group? How did you clarify your process so they would understand your thinking?
Why did you solve the problem this way?	How did you decide how to solve this problem?	What did you learn from the problem that helped you decide how to solve it?	Describe how you decided which steps and strategies to use to solve the problem.
If someone else were to solve this problem, what would you tell him or her?	If someone else were going to solve this problem, what should he or she look out for?	If someone else were to solve this problem, what tips would you give him or her?	If someone else were attempting to solve this problem, what advice or tips would you give this person?

Considering Ideas of Others

Skill Overview

Students listen to and read the mathematical thinking of others. By doing this, students gain insight into different perspectives. Students will learn that there are multiple ways to arrive at a correct answer and multiple ways of thinking about the same problem. Students discuss the work of others, asking relevant and helpful questions about their thinking, strategies, and solutions. Through this process, students will make connections between their own strategies and solutions and those implemented by others.

Students allow others to critique and analyze their work. They can then use this feedback to alter and improve their own work. By discussing mathematical problems and ideas with others, students are able to examine, refine, and validate their own thoughts and ideas. This dialogue and feedback mirrors how professionals and scholars discuss and evaluate their work.

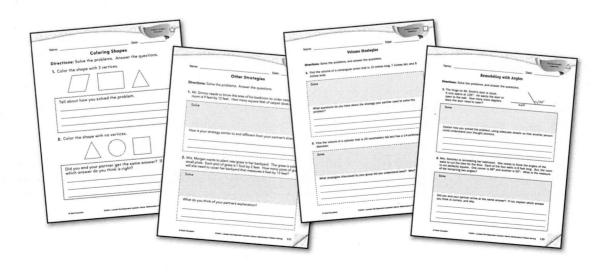

Implementing the Question Stems

This section includes 10 leveled, text-dependent question stems about considering the ideas of others. You can implement these question stems by connecting them to the mathematical concepts that you are studying in class.

It may seem as though using question stems would be easy, but it can be a complex task for teachers. To help you see how to implement these question stems in your classroom, this section includes student pages containing problems with sample text-dependent questions. Each of the four student pages illustrates a different complexity level.

Snapshot of Differentiating a Question

The chart below models how a single leveled question stem can be tied to mathematics problems at four complexity levels. This snapshot also gives a quick view of how the question stems differ based on the complexity levels. However, you can also see how the question stems link to one another.

	Question Stem	Example
☆	Tell about how you solved the problem.	Tell about how you added these numbers.
○	Explain how you solved the problem.	Explain how you solved the multiplication problem.
□	Explain how you solved the problem. Include enough details so another person could understand.	Explain how you solved for x. Include enough details so another person could understand.
△	Explain how you solved the problem, using adequate details so that another person could understand your thought process.	Explain how you solved the inequality, using adequate details so that another person could understand your thought process.

COMPLEXITY

LOW · HIGH

Considering Ideas of Others Question Stems

Use these question stems to develop your own questions for students.

Tell about how you solved the problem.

How did your partner solve the problem?

What is the same about how you and your partner solved the problem? What is different?

How did your partner explain his/her thinking?

What questions do you have about what your partner did?

Did you and your partner get the same answer? If not, which answer do you think is right?

What did your partner say that made you change your mind?

What steps will you try now that you have talked to your group?

Do you agree with what your partner said? Why or why not?

What question can you ask your partner about his/her thinking?

Name: _____ Date: _____

Coloring Shapes

Directions: Solve the problems. Answer the questions.

1. Color the shape with 3 vertices.

Tell about how you solved the problem.

_____

_____

_____

2. Color the shape with no vertices.

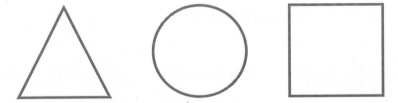

Did you and your partner get the same answer? If not, which answer do you think is right?

_____

_____

_____

Considering Ideas of Others Question Stems

Use these question stems to develop your own questions for students.

Explain how you solved the problem.

How did your partner solve the problem? Why do you think he/she chose that strategy?

How is your strategy similar to and different from your partner's strategy?

How did your partner explain his/her thinking about how to solve the problem?

What questions do you have about how your partner solved the problem?

Did you and your partner get the same answer? If not, which answer do you think is correct?

What information did your partner give that made you change your thinking?

Which strategy discussed by your group did you like best? Why?

What do you think of your partner's explanation?

What questions can you ask your partner to better understand how he/she solved the problem?

Name: _____ Date: _____

Other Strategies

Directions: Solve the problems. Answer the questions.

1. Mr. Simms needs to know the area of his bedroom to order carpet. The room is 9 feet by 12 feet. How many square feet of carpet does he need?

Solve

How is your strategy similar to and different from your partner's strategy?

_____

_____

2. Mrs. Morgan wants to plant new grass in her backyard. The grass is sold in small plots. Each plot of grass is 1 foot by 2 feet. How many plots of grass will she need to cover her backyard that measures 6 feet by 15 feet?

Solve

What do you think of your partner's explanation?

_____

_____

Considering Ideas of Others Question Stems

Use these question stems to develop your own questions for students.

Explain how you solved the problem. Include enough details so another person could understand.

Evaluate the strategy your partner used to solve the problem. Do you think there is a better way to solve the problem?

Compare and contrast your strategy and your partner's strategy.

Summarize how your partner explained his/her thinking about how to solve the problem.

What questions do you have about the strategy your partner used to solve the problem?

Did you and your partner get the same answer? If not, which answer do you think is correct, and why?

What information did your partner provide that made you change your thinking? Explain how it changed.

What strategies discussed by your group did you understand best? Why?

Evaluate your partner's explanation.

What questions can you ask your partner to better understand his/her strategy?

Name: _____ Date: _____

Volume Strategies

Directions: Solve the problems, and answer the questions.

1. Find the volume of a rectangular prism that is 15 inches long, 7 inches tall, and 8 inches wide.

> Solve
>
> What questions do you have about the strategy your partner used to solve the problem?
>
> _____
>
> _____
>
> _____

2. Find the volume of a cylinder that is 23 centimeters tall and has a 14-centimeter diameter.

> Solve
>
> What strategies discussed by your group did you understand best? Why?
>
> _____
>
> _____
>
> _____

Considering Ideas of Others Question Stems

Use these question stems to develop your own questions for students.

Explain how you solved the problem, using adequate details so that another person could understand your thought process.

Evaluate how your partner solved the problem. Explain why you think he/she chose that strategy, and evaluate if it is an efficient strategy for finding the solution.

Evaluate your strategy and your partner's strategy. Which strategy is more efficient?

Evaluate how your partner explained his/her thinking about the problem. Was he/she accurate, or were there errors that need to be fixed to solve the problem correctly?

Identify any questions you have about the strategies your partner used to solve the problem.

Did you and your partner arrive at the same answer? If not, explain which answer you think is correct, and why.

What feedback did your partner provide that made you change your thinking? Explain how it changed.

Evaluate the strategies your group discussed. Which strategy do you think is the most efficient way to solve the problem? Why?

Evaluate your partner's explanation. Include whether it is an efficient way to solve the problem.

What questions can you ask your partner to clarify his/her strategies?

Name: _____   Date: _____

Remodeling with Angles

Directions: Solve the problems, and answer the questions.

1. The hinge on Mr. Smith's door is stuck.
   It only opens to 125°. He wants the door to
   open to the wall. How many more degrees
   does the door need to open?

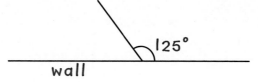

Solve

Explain how you solved the problem, using adequate details so that another person
could understand your thought process.

_____

_____

_____

2. Mrs. Sanchez is remodeling her bathroom. She needs to know the angles of the
   walls so that she can cut the tiles for the floor. Each of the four walls is 9 feet long.
   But, the room is not perfectly square. One corner is 88° and another is 92°. What is
   the measure of the remaining two angles?

Solve

Did you and your partner arrive at the same answer? If not, explain which answer
you think is correct, and why.

_____

_____

_____

Considering Ideas of Others K–12 Alignment

Use this chart to determine the best question stems for your different groups of students.

★	●	■	▲
Tell about how you solved the problem.	Explain how you solved the problem.	Explain how you solved the problem. Include enough details so another person could understand.	Explain how you solved the problem, using adequate details so that another person could understand your thought process.
How did your partner solve the problem?	How did your partner solve the problem? Why do you think he/she chose that strategy?	Evaluate the strategy your partner used to solve the problem. Do you think there is a better way to solve the problem?	Evaluate how your partner solved the problem. Explain why you think he/she chose that strategy, and evaluate if it is an efficient strategy for finding the solution.
What is the same about how you and your partner solved the problem? What is different?	How is your strategy similar to and different from your partner's strategy?	Compare and contrast your strategy and your partner's strategy.	Evaluate your strategy and your partner's strategy. Which strategy is more efficient?
How did your partner explain his/her thinking?	How did your partner explain his/her thinking about how to solve the problem?	Summarize how your partner explained his/her thinking about how to solve the problem.	Evaluate how your partner explained his/her thinking about the problem. Was he/she accurate, or were there errors that need to be fixed to solve the problem correctly?
What questions do you have about what your partner did?	What questions do you have about how your partner solved the problem?	What questions do you have about the strategy your partner used to solve the problem?	Identify any questions you have about the strategies your partner used to solve the problem.

Considering Ideas of Others K–12 Alignment (cont.)

★	●	■	▲
Did you and your partner get the same answer? If not, which answer do you think is right?	Did you and your partner get the same answer? If not, which answer do you think is correct?	Did you and your partner get the same answer? If not, which answer do you think is correct, and why?	Did you and your partner arrive at the same answer? If not, explain which answer you think is correct, and why.
What did your partner say that made you change your mind?	What information did your partner give that made you change your thinking?	What information did your partner provide that made you change your thinking? Explain how it changed.	What feedback did your partner provide that made you change your thinking? Explain how it changed.
What steps will you try now that you have talked to your group?	Which strategy discussed by your group did you like best? Why?	What strategies discussed by your group did you understand best? Why?	Evaluate the strategies your group discussed. Which strategy do you think is the most efficient way to solve the problem? Why?
Do you agree with what your partner said? Why or why not?	What do you think of your partner's explanation?	Evaluate your partner's explanation.	Evaluate your partner's explanation. Include whether it is an efficient way to solve the problem.
What question can you ask your partner about his/her thinking?	What questions can you ask your partner to better understand how he/she solved the problem?	What questions can you ask your partner to better understand his/her strategy?	What questions can you ask your partner to clarify his/her strategies?

Justifying Strategies, Processes, and Solutions

Skill Overview

Students explain orally and in writing why their strategies, processes, and solutions are reasonable and accurate. Students should first review the problem and confirm that they understand it. Then, they analyze whether they used an efficient and logical strategy to solve the problem. Students should also analyze the steps they followed to ensure that their process was logical and sequential. Finally, students evaluate whether their solutions are reasonable. If students find any errors in their work, they should revisit the problem, and try other strategies and processes until they are confident in their findings. Students then support, defend, and justify their reasoning and their solutions using compelling evidence. Students may present the problem a different way, break it into smaller parts, relate it to prior learning, find examples, or find counterexamples.

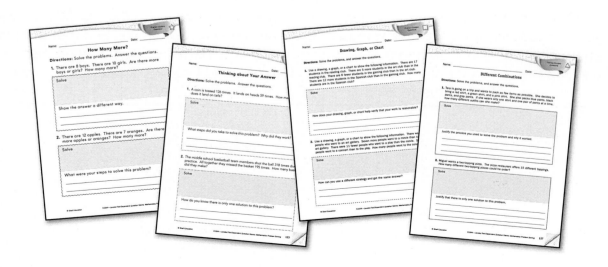

Implementing the Question Stems

This section includes 10 leveled, text-dependent question stems about justifying strategies, processes, and solutions. You can implement these question stems by connecting them to the mathematical concepts that you are studying in class.

It may seem as though using question stems would be easy, but it can be a complex task for teachers. To help you see how to implement these question stems in your classroom, this section includes student pages containing problems with sample text-dependent questions. Each of the four student pages illustrates a different complexity level.

Snapshot of Differentiating a Question

The chart below models how a single leveled question stem can be tied to mathematics problems at four complexity levels. This snapshot also gives a quick view of how the question stems differ based on the complexity levels. However, you can also see how the question stems link to one another.

	Question Stem	Example
☆	What were your steps to solve this problem?	What were your steps to subtract these numbers?
○	What steps did you take to solve this problem? Why did they work?	What steps did you take to add these fractions? Why did they work?
□	What process did you use to solve the problem, and why did it work?	What process did you use to find the surface area, and why did it work?
△	Justify the process you used to solve the problem and why it worked.	Justify the process you used to solve the linear equation and why it worked.

Justifying Strategies, Processes, and Solutions Question Stems

Use these question stems to develop your own questions for students.

Is there another answer? How do you know?

Show the answer a different way.

Does the way you solved the problem make sense? Why?

Can you solve the problem a different way? How?

What were your steps to solve this problem?

Why is the way you solved the problem the best way?

Is your answer right? How can you show it?

How does your drawing/graph/chart show that your answer is right?

What would be a wrong way to solve the problem? Why is it wrong?

What would a similar problem look like?

Name: _____ Date: _____

How Many More?

Directions: Solve the problems. Answer the questions.

1. There are 8 boys. There are 10 girls. Are there more boys or girls? How many more?

Solve

Show the answer a different way.

_____

_____

2. There are 12 apples. There are 7 oranges. Are there more apples or oranges? How many more?

Solve

What were your steps to solve this problem?

_____

_____

Justifying Strategies, Processes, and Solutions Question Stems

Use these question stems to develop your own questions for students.

How do you know there is only one solution to this problem?

How else can you show the solution?

Why does the strategy you used to solve the problem make sense?

What is another strategy you can use to solve this problem?

What steps did you take to solve this problem? Why did they work?

How can you show that your strategy was the best one to use?

How can you prove that your answer is correct?

How does your drawing/graph/chart show that your work is reasonable?

Give an example of an incorrect process. Why doesn't it work?

Create a similar problem, and use the same process to solve it.

Name: _____ Date: _____

Thinking about Your Answer

Directions: Solve the problems. Answer the questions.

1. A coin is tossed 126 times. It lands on heads 59 times. How many times does it land on tails?

Solve

What steps did you take to solve this problem? Why did they work?

_____

_____

2. The middle school basketball team members shot the ball 318 times during practice. All together, they missed the basket 195 times. How many baskets did they make?

Solve

How do you know there is only one solution to this problem?

_____

_____

Justifying Strategies, Processes, and Solutions Question Stems

Use these question stems to develop your own questions for students.

How can you prove that there is only one solution to this problem?

Explain another way to demonstrate the solution.

Explain why the strategy you used to solve the problem is efficient and logical.

How can you use a different strategy and get the same answer?

What process did you use to solve the problem, and why did it work?

How can you prove that you chose the best strategy to solve this problem?

Defend that your answer is correct.

How does your drawing/graph/chart help verify that your work is reasonable?

Give an example of an incorrect process, and contrast it with yours. What makes it incorrect, aside from the answer?

Create a similar problem, and use the same process to solve it. How does this prove that you used the correct process?

Name: _____ Date: _____

Drawing, Graph, or Chart

Directions: Solve the problems, and answer the questions.

1. Use a chart to show the following information. There are 17 students in the reading club. There are 5 more students in the art club than in the reading club. There are 6 fewer students in the gaming club than in the art club. There are 12 more students in the Spanish club than in the gaming club. How many students are in the Spanish club?

Solve

How does your chart help verify that your work is reasonable?

_____

_____

2. Use a chart to show the following information. There were 39 people who went to an art gallery. Seven more people went to a movie than to the art gallery. There were 11 fewer people who went to a play than the movie. Six more people went to a concert than to the play. How many people went to the concert?

Solve

How can you use a different strategy and get the same answer?

_____

_____

COMPLEXITY

LOW ★ ● ■ △ HIGH

Justifying Strategies, Processes, and Solutions Question Stems

Use these question stems to develop your own questions for students.

Defend the idea that there is only one solution to this problem.

Construct another way to demonstrate the solution to the problem.

What evidence is there from the problem to support the strategy you used to solve it?

Describe another strategy you can use to get the same answer. Which strategy is the most efficient?

Justify the process you used to solve the problem and why it worked.

How can you prove that you chose the most efficient and logical strategy to solve this problem?

Write a defense that explains how your answer is correct.

How does your drawing/graph/chart support your answer and verify that your work is reasonable?

Contrast your process with an incorrect one. What makes it incorrect, aside from the answer?

Create a similar problem, and use the same process to solve it. How does this validate your process?

Name: _____ Date: _____

Different Combinations

Directions: Solve the problems, and answer the questions.

1. Tara is going on a trip and wants to pack as few items as possible. She decides to bring a red shirt, a green shirt, and a pink shirt. She also packs blue pants, black pants, and gray pants. If she wears only one shirt and one pair of pants at a time, how many different outfits can she make?

Solve

Justify the process you used to solve the problem and why it worked.

_____

_____

_____

2. Miguel wants a two-topping pizza. The pizza restaurant offers 15 different toppings. How many different two-topping pizzas could he order?

Solve

Justify that there is only one solution to this problem.

_____

_____

_____

Justifying Strategies, Processes, and Solutions K–12 Alignment

Use this chart to determine the best question stems for your different groups of students.

★	●	■	▲
Is there another answer? How do you know?	How do you know there is only one solution to this problem?	How can you prove that there is only one solution to this problem?	Defend the idea that there is only one solution to this problem.
Show the answer a different way.	How else can you show the solution?	Explain another way to demonstrate the solution.	Construct another way to demonstrate the solution to the problem.
Does the way you solved the problem make sense? Why?	Why does the strategy you used to solve the problem make sense?	Explain why the strategy you used to solve the problem is efficient and logical.	What evidence is there from the problem to support the strategy you used to solve it?
Can you solve the problem a different way? How?	What is another strategy you can use to solve this problem?	How can you use a different strategy and get the same answer?	Describe another strategy you can use to get the same answer. Which strategy is the most efficient?
What were your steps to solve this problem?	What steps did you take to solve this problem? Why did they work?	What process did you use to solve the problem, and why did it work?	Justify the process you used to solve the problem and why it worked.

Justifying Strategies, Processes, and Solutions
K–12 Alignment (cont.)

★	●	■	▲
Why is the way you solved the problem the best way?	How can you show that your strategy was the best one to use?	How can you prove that you chose the best strategy to solve this problem?	How can you prove that you chose the most efficient and logical strategy to solve this problem?
Is your answer right? How can you show it?	How can you prove that your answer is correct?	Defend that your answer is correct.	Write a defense that explains how your answer is correct.
How does your drawing/graph/chart show that your answer is right?	How does your drawing/graph/chart show that your work is reasonable?	How does your drawing/graph/chart help verify that your work is reasonable?	How does your drawing/graph/chart support your answer and verify that your work is reasonable?
What would be a wrong way to solve the problem? Why is it wrong?	Give an example of an incorrect process. Why doesn't it work?	Give an example of an incorrect process, and contrast it with yours. What makes it incorrect, aside from the answer?	Contrast your process with an incorrect one. What makes it incorrect, aside from the answer?
What would a similar problem look like?	Create a similar problem, and use the same process to solve it.	Create a similar problem, and use the same process to solve it. How does this prove that you used the correct process?	Create a similar problem, and use the same process to solve it. How does this validate your process?

Creating Word Problems

Skill Overview

Students use their imaginations, creativity, and mathematical knowledge to write interesting and challenging word problems to solve and share with others. They use grade-appropriate writing, content-area vocabulary, and mathematical skills to write problems that can be solved. Students may model problems after similar word problems from textbooks or from other resources. Students listen to and read word problems written by others and share their own.

This skill not only integrates language arts into mathematics, but it also strengthens and reinforces students' mathematical skills. Students may try several variations before creating problems that can be solved, which requires extensive knowledge of the mathematical concepts involved. They must verify the correct answers to their problems and ensure that there is sufficient information to solve their problems. They may also be asked to explain how to solve their problems step by step.

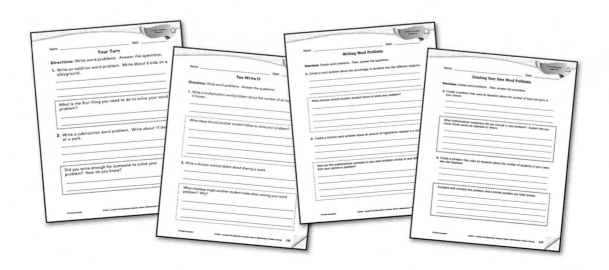

Implementing the Question Stems

This section includes 10 leveled, text-dependent question stems about creating word problems. You can implement these question stems by connecting them to the mathematical concepts that you are studying in class.

It may seem as though using question stems would be easy, but it can be a complex task for teachers. To help you see how to implement these question stems in your classroom, this section includes student pages containing problems with sample text-dependent questions. Each of the four student pages illustrates a different complexity level.

Snapshot of Differentiating a Question

The chart below models how a single leveled question stem can be tied to mathematics problems at four complexity levels. This snapshot also gives a quick view of how the question stems differ based on the complexity levels. However, you can also see how the question stems link to one another.

	Question Stem	Example
☆	How should a student solve your problem?	How should a student solve your problem?
○	What steps should another student follow to solve your problem?	What steps should a student follow to find the product?
□	What process should another student follow to solve your problem?	What process should another student follow to solve your equation?
△	Describe the process another student should follow to solve your problem.	Describe the process another student should follow to solve for *x*.

Creating Word Problems Question Stems

Use these question stems to develop your own questions for students.

What is the first step to solve your word problem?

What is the same about your word problem and your partner's?

How is this word problem the same as a different problem?

Why did you use _____ (*mathematical concept*) in your problem?

What mathematical words did you use in your problem?

How should another student solve your problem?

What mistakes do you think a student might make when solving your problem?

Did you write enough for someone to solve your problem? How do you know?

How would you solve your partner's word problem?

How can you make your word problem harder?

Name: _____ Date: _____

Your Turn

Directions: Write word problems. Answer the questions.

1. Write an addition word problem. Write about 6 kids on a playground.

_____

_____

_____

What is the first step to solve your word problem?

_____

_____

_____

2. Write a subtraction word problem. Write about 11 dogs at a park.

_____

_____

_____

Did you write enough for someone to solve your problem? How do you know?

_____

_____

_____

Creating Word Problems Question Stems

Use these question stems to develop your own questions for students.

What steps are needed to solve your word problem?

What is the same about the mathematical concepts in your word problem and your partner's? What is different?

How is this word problem similar to another one that you have solved?

Why did you include these mathematical concepts in your problem?

What mathematical vocabulary did you use in your problem?

What steps should another student follow to solve your problem?

What mistakes might another student make when solving your word problem? Why?

Is there enough information in your word problem for someone to solve it? How do you know?

Explain how to solve your partner's word problem.

What could you do to make your word problem more difficult? Explain your thinking.

Name: _____   Date: _____

You Write It

Directions: Write word problems. Answer the questions.

1. Write a multiplication word problem about the number of art supplies in boxes.

_____

_____

> What steps should another student follow to solve your problem?
>
> _____
>
> _____
>
> _____
>
> _____

2. Write a division word problem about sharing a snack.

_____

_____

> What mistakes might another student make when solving your word problem? Why?
>
> _____
>
> _____
>
> _____

LOW ★ ● □ ▲ HIGH

Creating Word Problems Question Stems

Use these question stems to develop your own questions for students.

What processes are needed to solve your word problem?

How are the mathematical concepts in your word problem similar to and different from your partner's problem?

Describe similarities and differences between this problem and another problem you have solved.

Explain why you included these mathematical concepts in your problem. What concepts did you not include?

What mathematical vocabulary did you include in your problem? What other vocabulary could you have used?

What process should another student follow to solve your problem?

Describe any common mistakes another student may make when solving your word problem and why.

Did you include enough information in your word problem for someone to solve it? How do you know?

Explain the steps to solve your partner's word problem.

List suggestions to make your word problem more difficult. Why do these suggestions make it harder?

Name: _____ Date: _____

Writing Word Problems

Directions: Create word problems. Then, answer the questions.

1. Create a word problem about the percentage of students who like different subjects.

_____

_____

_____

What process should another student follow to solve your problem?

_____

_____

_____

_____

2. Create a fraction word problem about an amount of ingredients needed in a recipe.

_____

_____

_____

How are the mathematical concepts in your word problem similar to and different from your partner's problem?

_____

_____

_____

_____

Creating Word Problems Question Stems

Use these question stems to develop your own questions for students.

How do you know what processes are needed to solve your problem? Include specific examples in your response.

Compare and contrast the mathematical concepts in your word problem and your partner's word problem.

Compare and contrast this problem and a similar problem you have solved.

Explain why you included these mathematical concepts in your problem as opposed to others.

What mathematical vocabulary did you include in your problem? Explain why you chose those words as opposed to others.

Describe the process another student should follow to solve your problem.

Describe any common mistakes another student may make when solving your word problem. What misconceptions might these mistakes reveal?

Use evidence from your problem to prove that you included sufficient information for someone to solve it.

Use step-by-step instructions to explain how to solve your partner's word problem.

List suggestions to increase the difficulty of your word problem. Explain why these suggestions make it more difficult.

Name: _____ Date: _____

Creating Your Own Word Problems

Directions: Create word problems. Then, answer the questions.

1. Create a problem that uses an equation about the number of boys and girls in your school.

_____

_____

_____

What mathematical vocabulary did you include in your problem? Explain why you chose those words as opposed to others.

_____

_____

_____

2. Create a problem that uses an equation about the number of students in your class who like baseball.

_____

_____

_____

Compare and contrast this problem and a similar problem you have solved.

_____

_____

_____

Creating Word Problems K–12 Alignment

Use this chart to determine the best question stems for your different groups of students.

★	●	■	▲
What is the first step to solve your word problem?	What steps are needed to solve your word problem?	What processes are needed to solve your word problem?	How do you know what processes are needed to solve your problem? Include specific examples in your response.
What is the same about your word problem and your partner's?	What is the same about the mathematical concepts in your word problem and your partner's? What is different?	How are the mathematical concepts in your word problem similar to and different from your partner's problem?	Compare and contrast the mathematical concepts in your word problem and your partner's word problem.
How is this word problem the same as a different problem?	How is this word problem similar to another one that you have solved?	Describe similarities and differences between this problem and another problem you have solved.	Compare and contrast this problem and a similar problem you have solved.
Why did you use _____ (*mathematical concept*) in your problem?	Why did you include these mathematical concepts in your problem?	Explain why you included these mathematical concepts in your problem. What concepts did you not include?	Explain why you included these mathematical concepts in your problem as opposed to others.
What mathematical words did you use in your problem?	What mathematical vocabulary did you use in your problem?	What mathematical vocabulary did you include in your problem? What other vocabulary could you have used?	What mathematical vocabulary did you include in your problem? Explain why you chose those words as opposed to others.

Creating Word Problems K–12 Alignment (cont.)

★	○	▢	▲
How should a student solve your problem?	What steps should another student follow to solve your problem?	What process should another student follow to solve your problem?	Describe the process another student should follow to solve your problem.
What mistakes do you think another student might make when solving your problem?	What mistakes might another student make when solving your word problem? Why?	Describe any common mistakes another student may make when solving your word problem and why.	Describe any common mistakes another student may make when solving your word problem. What misconceptions might these mistakes reveal?
Did you write enough for someone to solve your problem? How do you know?	Is there enough information in your word problem for someone to solve it? How do you know?	Did you include enough information in your word problem for someone to solve it? How do you know?	Use evidence from your problem to prove that you included sufficient information for someone to solve it.
How would you solve your partner's word problem?	Explain how to solve your partner's word problem.	Explain the steps to solve your partner's word problem.	Use step-by-step instructions to explain how to solve your partner's word problem.
How can you make your word problem harder?	What could you do to make your word problem more difficult? Explain your thinking.	List suggestions to make your word problem more difficult. Why do these suggestions make it harder?	List suggestions to increase the difficulty of your word problem. Explain why these suggestions make it more difficult.

Discovering Mathematics in the Real World

Skill Overview

It is important for students to realize that mathematics is part of their daily lives. Students can strengthen their skills by discovering the real-life applications of mathematics in the world around them. This helps students become more motivated and engaged in solving interesting and challenging problems.

There are many mathematical skills, including measurement, time, and fractions, that students can identify as they help cook. Students can explore addition, subtraction, and multiplication as they learn to budget and save money they earn from allowances or part-time jobs. Working in a garden may provide opportunities to practice multiplication, division, and geometry. Students apply the mathematics they know and are able to do by solving real-life problems and recognizing that mathematics is essential in their daily lives.

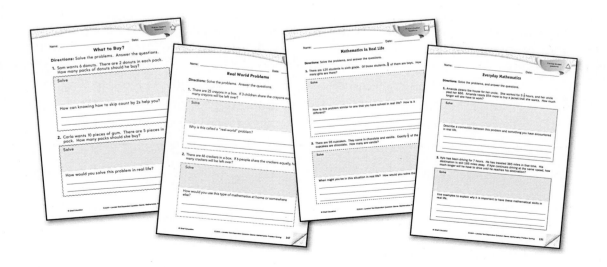

Implementing the Question Stems

This section includes 10 leveled, text-dependent question stems about mathematics in the real world. You can implement these question stems by connecting them to the mathematical concepts that you are studying in class.

It may seem as though using question stems would be easy, but it can be a complex task for teachers. To help you see how to implement these question stems in your classroom, this section includes student pages containing problems with sample text-dependent questions. Each of the four student pages illustrates a different complexity level.

Snapshot of Differentiating a Question

The chart below models how a single leveled question stem can be tied to mathematics problems at four complexity levels. This snapshot also gives a quick view of how the question stems differ based on the complexity levels. However, you can also see how the question stems link to one another.

	Question Stem	Example
☆	How can knowing _____ (*mathematical concept*) help you?	How can knowing how to add help you?
○	How can knowing _____ (*mathematical concept*) make your life better?	How can knowing division make your life better?
☐	Explain how knowing _____ (*mathematical concept*) could improve your daily life.	Explain how knowing how to convert fractions to decimals could improve your daily life.
△	Describe how knowing _____ (*mathematical concept*) assists you or someone you know in real life.	Describe how knowing how to solve for an unknown variable assists you or someone you know in real life.

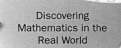

Discovering Mathematics in the Real World Question Stems

Use these question stems to develop your own questions for students.

How would you solve this problem in real life?

What does this problem make you think of?

Have you solved a problem like this in real life? Tell about it.

When would you use _____ (*mathematical concept*) at home?

What kind of problem could help you do a chore?

How can knowing _____ (*mathematical concept*) help you?

How could you make this problem about your life?

Who might have a problem like this one in real life?

Why is it good to know how to do this kind of problem?

Could this be called a "real-world" problem? Why or why not?

Name: _____   Date: _____

What to Buy?

Directions: Solve the problems. Answer the questions.

1. Sam wants 6 donuts. There are 2 donuts in each pack. How many packs of donuts should he buy?

Solve

How can knowing how to skip count by 2s help you?

_____

_____

2. Carla wants 10 pieces of gum. There are 5 pieces in each pack. How many packs should she buy?

Solve

How would you solve this problem in real life?

_____

_____

Discovering Mathematics in the Real World Question Stems

Use these question stems to develop your own questions for students.

If you were in this situation in real life, how would you solve it?

What connection can you make to this problem?

How is this like a problem you have solved in real life?

How would you use this type of mathematics at home or somewhere else?

How could mathematics make a chore or a task easier?

How can knowing _____ (*mathematical concept*) make your life better?

How can you change this problem to make it about something familiar to you?

Who do you know that might have a problem like this in real life? How could he or she solve it?

Why is it important to be able to do this type of problem in real life?

Why is this called a "real-world" problem?

Name: _____ Date: _____

Real-World Problems

Directions: Solve the problems. Answer the questions.

1. There are 25 crayons in a box. If 3 children share the crayons equally, how many crayons will be left over?

Solve

Why is this called a "real-world" problem?

_____

_____

2. There are 46 crackers in a box. If 6 people share the crackers equally, how many crackers will be left over?

Solve

How would you use this type of mathematics at home or somewhere else?

_____

_____

Discovering Mathematics in the Real World Question Stems

Use these question stems to develop your own questions for students.

When might you be in this situation in real life? How would you solve the problem?

Explain a connection between this problem and something you have seen in real life.

How is this problem similar to one that you have solved in real life? How is it different?

Describe when and how you would use this type of mathematics in everyday life.

Explain how mathematics could help you complete a chore or a task more easily.

Explain how knowing _____ (*mathematical concept*) could improve your daily life.

Rewrite this problem to reflect a situation that is familiar to you.

Who do you know that might encounter a situation like this in real life? How could he or she solve it?

Why is it important to have these mathematical skills in real life?

Why is this called a "real-world" problem? When might someone solve a problem like this?

Name: _____ Date: _____

Mathematics in Real Life

Directions: Solve the problems, and answer the questions.

1. There are 120 students in sixth grade. Of those students, $\frac{5}{8}$ of them are boys. How many girls are there?

Solve

How is this problem similar to one that you have solved in real life? How is it different?

_____

_____

_____

2. There are 95 cupcakes. They come in chocolate and vanilla. Exactly $\frac{1}{5}$ of the cupcakes are chocolate. How many are vanilla?

Solve

When might you be in this situation in real life? How would you solve the problem?

_____

_____

_____

Discovering Mathematics in the Real World Question Stems

Use these question stems to develop your own questions for students.

Describe a scenario where you might be in this situation in real life. How would you solve the problem?

Describe a connection between this problem and something you have encountered in real life.

Compare and contrast this problem to a similar real-life problem that you have solved.

Explain how this type of mathematics could be useful in everyday life. Give a specific example of how you could use it.

Explain how a type of mathematics could help you complete an everyday chore or task more easily or more efficiently.

Describe how knowing _____ (*mathematical concept*) assists you or someone you know in real life.

Rewrite this problem to reflect a situation that is familiar to you. How can you connect with the problem better now?

Who do you know that might encounter a similar situation in real life? Describe the ways that he/she could solve it.

Use examples to explain why it is important to have these mathematical skills in real life.

Why is this called a "real-world" problem? When might someone encounter a problem or situation similar to this?

Name: _____ Date: _____

Everyday Mathematics

Directions: Solve the problems, and answer the questions.

1. Amanda cleans the house for her uncle. She worked for $5\frac{1}{2}$ hours, and her uncle paid her $66. Amanda needs $54 more to buy a jacket that she wants. How much longer will she have to work?

> Solve
>
> ---
>
> Describe a connection between this problem and something you have encountered in real life.
>
> _____
>
> _____
>
> _____

2. Kyle has been driving for 7 hours. He has traveled 385 miles in that time. His destination is still 165 miles away. If Kyle continues driving at the same speed, how much longer will he have to drive until he reaches his destination?

> Solve
>
> ---
>
> Use examples to explain why it is important to have these mathematical skills in real life.
>
> _____
>
> _____
>
> _____

Discovering Mathematics in the Real World K–12 Alignment

Use this chart to determine the best question stems for your different groups of students.

★	●	■	▲
How would you solve this problem in real life?	If you were in this situation in real life, how would you solve it?	When might you be in this situation in real life? How would you solve the problem?	Describe a scenario where you might be in this situation in real life. How would you solve the problem?
What does this problem make you think of?	What connection can you make to this problem?	Explain a connection between this problem and something you have seen in real life.	Describe a connection between this problem and something you have encountered in real life.
Have you solved a problem like this in real life? Tell about it.	How is this like a problem you have solved in real life?	How is this problem similar to one that you have solved in real life? How is it different?	Compare and contrast this problem to a similar real-life problem that you have solved.
When would you use _____ (mathematical concept) at home?	How would you use this type of mathematics at home or somewhere else?	Describe when and how you would use this type of mathematics in everyday life.	Explain how this type of mathematics could be useful in everyday life. Give a specific example of how you could use it.
What kind of problem could help you do a chore?	How could mathematics make a chore or a task easier?	Explain how mathematics could help you complete a chore or a task more easily.	Explain how a type of mathematics could help you complete an everyday chore or task more easily or more efficiently.

Discovering Mathematics in the Real World
K–12 Alignment *(cont.)*

★	●	■	▲
How can knowing _____ (*mathematical concept*) help you?	How can knowing _____ (*mathematical concept*) make your life better?	Explain how knowing _____ (*mathematical concept*) could improve your daily life.	Describe how knowing _____ (*mathematical concept*) assists you or someone you know in real life.
How could you make this problem about your life?	How can you change this problem to make it about something familiar to you?	Rewrite this problem to reflect a situation that is familiar to you.	Rewrite this problem to reflect a situation that is familiar to you. How can you connect with the problem better now?
Who might have a problem like this one in real life?	Who do you know that might have a problem like this in real life? How could he or she solve it?	Who do you know that might encounter a situation like this in real life? How could he or she solve it?	Who do you know that might encounter a similar situation in real life? Describe the ways that he/she could solve it.
Why is it good to know how to do this kind of problem?	Why is it important to be able to do this type of problem in real life?	Why is it important to have these mathematical skills in real life?	Use examples to explain why it is important to have these mathematical skills in real life.
Could this be called a "real-world" problem? Why or why not?	Why is this called a "real-world" problem?	Why is this called a "real-world" problem? When might someone solve a problem like this?	Why is this called a "real-world" problem? When might someone encounter a problem or situation similar to this?

Answer Key

Answers for all mathematical problems are listed. Responses to TDQs will vary. Sample responses are provided.

Planning Subtraction (page 13)

1. 2 pieces are left. Yes. I could draw a picture because that could show what is happening.

2. 5 toys are left. My answer makes sense because there are 3 fewer toys on the desk than before.

Finding Fractions (page 15)

1. $\frac{4}{12}$ or $\frac{1}{3}$ of the balls are red. From the problem, I know that there are 12 balls total. Four of them are red.

2. $\frac{4}{20}$ or $\frac{1}{5}$ of the markers are blue. First, I will add the orange and purple markers. Then, I will subtract that number from the total to find the number of blue markers. Finally, I will place that number over 20 to form a fraction.

Planning with Fractions (page 17)

1. Matteo is taller than Daniel. When I solve the problem. I will have found the relative heights of Matteo and Daniel.

2. 16 inches. My solution is reasonable because 16 is $\frac{1}{3}$ of 48 inches.

Order Fulfillment (page 19)

1. Neveah needs 2,448 bags. Knowing the pounds of beads and how much each bag holds is critical. The number of colors is not needed. It is not needed because the color doesn't affect the amount of beads that will fit in a bag.

2. Miguel can fill 202 bags. I will have found how many bags can be filled with this amount of coffee.

Time to Measure (page 25)

1. 5 counters. The unit of measurement I should use is counters or paper clips.

2. 7 counters. I know my answer is correct because the shoe stops after seven counters.

Measuring Up (page 27)

1. 9 bows. I need to convert yards to inches because that is the unit the bows are measured in.

2. 4.08 meters. Knowing there are 100 cm in a meter helps me because then I can convert the length to meters to solve the problem.

Mind the Units (page 29)

1. 7 yards. The question is asking for yards, so I should attach that unit to the answer.

2. 7 packs of streamers. The numbers in the problem guide me, because I know that I will need to convert the units before solving the problem. First, I will convert the numbers to meters. Then, I will add all four walls, and then I will divide to see how many packs he needs.

Household Mathematics (page 31)

1. Yes, the rug will fit. I had to convert the units before finding a solution because the circumference is in feet and the distance between the couch and TV is in inches.

2. No, the garden box will not fit. The numbers are related because 98 inches equals 8.17 feet, which is greater than 8 feet.

Hands and Legs (page 37)

1. 8 legs. I can use counters to solve this problem.

2. 6 hands. My picture shows 3 people, and each has 2 hands.

Time to Exercise (page 39)

1. 63 miles. I can use a picture to show how many miles she runs in a week. Then, I can multiply by 3 to get the total.

2. 120 miles. I can prove my answer by representing one bike ride of 5 miles.

Saving Up (page 41)

1. $4,470. I plan to figure out how much money was donated by each group of people and then add the amounts together.

2. $267. I can connect this type of problem to figuring out how much money individuals need to pitch in to buy a large item.

Answer Key (cont.)

Fractional Planning (page 43)

1. 105 cookies. I can organize the information by figuring out how many cookies were in $\frac{1}{3}$ and then multiplying by 3 to find the total. It helps me because I can think in terms of whole cookies rather than fractions.

2. 470 trading cards.

94	94	94	94	94

   A drawing is the most efficient tool because it helps me to see whether the answer makes sense.

What's the Weight? (page 49)

1. Verify measurement. I can use a scale to help me.

2. Verify measurement. I estimated 10 grams. Yes, my answer was close.

Classroom Measurement (page 51)

1. Verify measurement. I can use a yardstick to solve the problem.

2. Verify measurement. A balance would not help me because it measures weight, not length.

Tools in School (page 53)

1. Verify measurement. I could use a tape measure to find the solution. It is appropriate because it measures length.

2. Verify measurement. I need to measure the length and width of the desk and then multiply them together. I need to be able to measure and multiply. I need a yardstick or tape measure.

Geometry at School (page 55)

1. Verify measurement. A ruler is the most effective tool because it measures length and is the right size.

2. Verify measurement. Estimation can help me determine if my solution is reasonable because I can compare it to my estimate.

Animal Fun (page 61)

1. 4 birds. You need to add because another bird joins the ones that are there.

2. 4 cats. Knowing that I had to subtract helped me solve the problem.

Problems with Presents (page 63)

1. 42 + 16 + 8 = 66 cards. You can switch the addends to find the sum because of the commutative property.

2. (27 + 2) − 3 = 26 stuffed animals. I can rearrange the numbers to (2 + 27) − 3 and still get 26.

Finding Properties (page 65)

1. $112. Using the distributive property doesn't help me solve the problem because there are only two numbers being multiplied.

2. 140 items. First, I will find out how many toys he needs. Then, I will find out how many games he needs. Then, I will add them together. I can use the commutative property while adding and multiplying.

School Lunches (page 67)

1. 965 lunches. I will multiply 193 by 5. I can use the commutative property.

2. 476 lunches. Using the distributive property, I could solve the problem by (136 ÷ 2) x (2 + 5). This is more efficient because there are fewer calculations.

Add it Up (page 73)

1. 5 kids. I draw both groups of kids. Then, I will count how many there are.

2. 7 birds. I knew that I need to add because of the word *more*.

How Much Time? (page 75)

1. 200 minutes (or 3 hours and 20 minutes). The strategy that will work best is to make a chart that shows Mindi's swim practice for a week.

2. 210 minutes (or three and a half hours). I could also solve the problem by writing an equation. One week + 3 (45 + 25)

Thinking about Ages (page 77)

1. Daniel will be 23 years old. Writing an equation would work best. Since Allison is two years younger, 21 + 2 = 23.

2. Maria will be 15 years old. The words *older* and *will be* helped me figure out what strategy to use.

Answer Key (cont.)

Mystery Jars (page 79)

1. 48 gumdrops. Logical reasoning is the best strategy because $\frac{1}{2}$ is twice as much as $\frac{1}{4}$.

2. 33 orange marbles. I first made a chart to solve the problem, and then I drew a picture. Both required me to read the problem carefully. Using a chart helped me to better organize the information.

Tens and Ones (page 85)

1. 12 years old. I could also draw tens and ones to solve the problem.

2. 23 rocks. The hardest part was that the values were given out of order. I had to rearrange the numbers to figure it out.

Number Riddles (page 87)

1. 49. I can ask: *What is 5 less than 9?*

2. 28. Another problem using the same steps is: I *am a number. The digit in my ones place is 5 more than the digit in my tens place. The digit in my tens place is 3. What number am I?* (38)

Making Up Numbers (page 89)

1. 98,632. Guess and check would not solve the problem effectively because you would have to guess many numbers (62,389 and 23,689 for example) before finding the largest one.

2. 12,479. I am exploring place value because I need to know how place value affects my answer. For example, 10,000 is smaller than 80,000.

Exponential Height (page 91)

1. 81 feet long. A similar problem is: *A gray whale is about 7^2 feet long. How long is it in standard notation?* (49 feet long)

2. 243 feet tall. Another way to solve the problem is to draw a picture. That would not be as efficient because it would take longer.

I Scream for Ice Cream (page 97)

1. Most kids like chocolate. I looked at the graph and compared the number of cones in each flavor.

2. 4 kids. I can best show my thinking by explaining how I solved the problem. I solved it by finding strawberry on the graphs. Then, I counted how many cones there were.

Fishing Trip (page 99)

1. 5 more fish. I looked at the graph to see that Raj caught 25 fish, and Karen caught 20. I then subtracted Karen's amount from Raj's.

2. 18 fish. I decided to look at the graph and saw that Amelia caught between 15 and 20 fish. It looked closer to 20, so I thought 18 was the best answer.

Battle of the Band (page 101)

1. 150 minutes. The problem is asking how long the longest concert was. To solve it, you need to look at the stem and leaf plot and determine that the largest stem is 15. The largest, and only, leaf is 0. Therefore, the longest concert was 150 minutes.

2. The concert is not a good value because it is shorter than all 20 concerts Emily investigated. I explained my thinking and process by pointing out that an expensive concert should be longer than average to be a good value. Since the shortest concert was 90 minutes, this is not a good value.

Calculating Coordinates (page 103)

1.

x	0	1	2	3	4	11
y	0	2	4	6	8	22

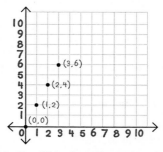

I decided to fill in the points already represented on the coordinate plane and then figure out the pattern on the table for the missing ones.

2. $y = 36$. The strategy I used was to find a pattern such as $x = 2y$. This is the best strategy because it allows you to quickly calculate any ordered pair.

Answer Key (cont.)

Coloring Shapes (page 109)

1. The triangle should be colored. I solved the problem by counting the vertices on each shape.

2. The circle should be colored. My partner and I got the same answer.

Other Strategies (page 111)

1. 108 square feet. I used an equation, and my partner drew a picture and then used an equation. The equations were the same.

2. 45 plots of grass. My partner did a good job explaining that 45 plots of grass would fill a backyard measuring 6 by 15 feet.

Volume Strategies (page 113)

1. 840 cubic inches. I want to know why my partner drew a rectangular prism and didn't just use the equation for volume.

2. 1,011.08 cubic centimeters. The strategies I understand best were using an equation and drawing a picture. I understand these best because I have used both strategies before.

Remodeling with Angles (page 115)

1. 55°. I subtracted how much the door could open (125°) from the measure of a straight line (180°). This represents the line of the wall.

2. 88° and 92°. My partner and I arrived at the same answers because we know that opposite angles must add up to 180°.

How Many More? (page 121)

1. There are 2 more girls than boys. Another way to show the answer is: 10 girls – 8 boys = 2 more girls.

2. There are 5 more apples. To solve the problem, I subtracted the number of oranges from the number of apples.

Thinking About Your Answer (page 123)

1. 67 times. I subtracted 59 from 129 to get the number of times it landed on tails. This worked because there are only two sides to a coin.

2. 123 baskets. I know there is only one solution to the problem because the team either made the basket or they did not. By subtracting the number of times they missed, we have the number of times they made a basket.

Drawing, Graph, or Chart (page 125)

1. 28 students. My chart helped me because it let me solve the problem one step at a time, and it let me check my work.

2. 41 people. I can create equations to represent the different events. As I solve for the first unknown, I can use that number to solve the next one.

Different Combinations (page 127)

1. 9 outfits. I drew a picture to represent each item. I used letters to represent the colors. Then, I listed the different combinations and counted them. This worked because it let me see if there was anything I missed.

2. 105 pizzas. There is only one solution because combination problems only have one solution.

Your Turn (page 133)

1. There are 6 kids on the playground. Three kids join them. How many kids are on the playground now? The first step to solve my word problem is to draw six kids.

2. There are 11 dogs at the park. Six dogs leave. How many dogs are left? I wrote enough for someone to solve it because I said how many dogs there were and how many left.

You Write It (page 135)

1. There are 9 boxes of paintbrushes with 20 brushes inside each box. How many paintbrushes are there? To solve my problem, another student should multiply the number of brushes by the number of boxes.

2. There are 2 boxes of 12 cookies each. How many cookies could 4 friends have if they share the cookies equally? Another student might forget to add the total number of cookies before dividing because they could think there are 12 cookies.

Answer Key *(cont.)*

Writing Word Problems (page 137)

1. 500 students were asked to choose their favorite subject. If 18% chose science, 32% chose language arts, 10% chose history, and the rest chose mathematics, how many students chose mathematics? To solve my problem, a student should add the percentages together and then subtract that from 100. Then, the student should divide by .12.

2. To make a salad, add $2\frac{1}{4}$ cups lettuce, 1 cup chopped apples, $\frac{1}{4}$ cup cranberries, and $\frac{1}{8}$ cup salad dressing. How much of the ingredients do you need to make a half salad of each? The mathematical concepts are similar because we both wrote fraction word problems about recipes. They are different because my problem involves division, and my partner's involves addition.

Create Your Own Word Problems (page 139)

1. There are 250 students in the school. $\frac{3}{5}$ of them are boys. What equation can be written to represent the percent of girls? The mathematical vocabulary I included are *equation* and *percent*. I chose those words because I wanted the person to write an equation involving percents.

2. About 10% of the students in my class like baseball. If there are 32 students in my class about, how many like baseball? This is similar to other problems I have solved because you have to round the answer to get to a whole number.

What to Buy? (page 145)

1. 3 packs. Knowing how to skip count by 2s helps me count more easily.

2. 2 packs. In real life, I would skip count until I got to the number I wanted.

Real-World Problems (page 147)

1. 1 crayon left over. This is a "real world" problem because it could happen in real life. Someone would want to know this to make sure everyone had an equal amount.

2. 4 crackers left over. I would use this type of mathematics at home to figure out how many servings I could eat before I ran out.

Mathematics in Real Life (page 149)

1. 45 girls. This problem is similar to other fraction problems that I have solved. It is different because the numbers and fractions are different.

2. 76 cupcakes. I might solve this problem in real life if I knew that only $\frac{1}{5}$ of people liked chocolate, and I was trying to plan for a party. To solve the problem I would find out how many people like chocolate and subtract that from the number attending.

Everyday Mathematics (page 151)

1. 4.5 hours. I wanted to save up for a car. I had to figure out how long it would take me to save up enough to buy it.

2. 3 hours. This is an important skill because you need to be able to estimate when you will arrive at a location or figure out how long it will take to get there.

Problem-Solving Strategies

Draw a picture or diagram.	Make a table or list.	Use a number sentence or formula.
		$10 + 4 = 14$ $A = l \times w$

Make a model.	Look for a pattern.	Act it out.
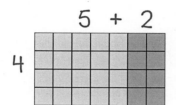	 **3, 6, 9, 12, 15,** __18__	

Solve a simpler problem.	Work backward.	Use logical reasoning.
$7 + 6$ $7 + 3 + 3$ $(7 + 3) + 3$ $10 + 3 = 13$	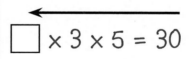 $\Box \times 3 \times 5 = 30$	

Guess and check.	Create a graph.	Use concrete objects.
$2 \times \Box + 5 = 13$ $2 \times 4 + 5 = 13$ $13 = 13$ Yes!	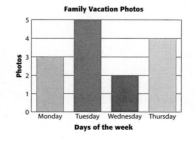	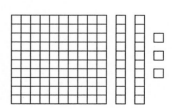 base-ten blocks

Notes